# Everyday
# TRAIL RIDING

## Eliza R. L. McGraw

Sterling Publishing Co., Inc.

New York

# For Macie

Unless otherwise noted, all photographs are by Onawa M. Cutshall

**Library of Congress Cataloging-in-Publication Data**

10 9 8 7 6 5 4 3 2 1

Published by Sterling Publishing Co., Inc.
387 Park Avenue South, New York, NY 10016
Copyright © 2005 by Eliza R. L. McGraw
Distributed in Canada by Sterling Publishing
ᶜ/ₒ Canadian Manda Group, 165 Dufferin Street
Toronto, Ontario, Canada M6K 3H6
Distributed in Great Britain by Chrysalis Books Group PLC
The Chrysalis Building, Bramley Road, London W10 6SP, England
Distributed in Australia by Capricorn Link (Australia) Pty. Ltd.
P.O. Box 704, Windsor, NSW 2756, Australia

*Printed in China*
*All rights reserved*

Sterling ISBN 1-4027-1662-1

For information about custom editions, special sales, premium and
corporate purchases, please contact Sterling Special Sales
Department at 800-805-5489 or specialsales@sterlingpub.com.

# Contents

# Acknowledgments

The writing of *Everyday Trail Riding* has been a group project in some ways, and I owe an enormous debt to everyone who helped me see it through.

Many thanks to the horses and riders who allowed themselves to be photographed for this book, and to the Maryland farm owners who provided the settings. Special thanks to Callithea Farm, the North Fork School of Equitation, Laurie Ridgeway, and the staff at Schooley Mill Park. Even with a newborn baby at home, Onawa Cutshall worked very hard to get all the right pictures.

Thanks to all my trail-riding companions over the years, especially Vicky Haber, Sheri Tigue, Kitson Flynn, Beth Evans, and Bruce Thompson. More thanks to George Sengstack, Jennifer Duncan, Monocacy Equine Veterinary Associates, and Brett Reilly. They have helped me care for my horse Romeo, who has carried me on so many trail rides.

My husband, Adam, has been trail riding with me in places from Arizona to Gettysburg. He has helped with this project by supporting both my riding and writing with visits to the barn and computer help. I am also very grateful to Madelyn Larsen, my agent and editor, who has seen this project through from the beginning and has spent as much time on it as I have.

My family was very helpful as I wrote, keeping me going with babysitting and encouragement. My mother, father, Jim, Gena, Abby, Kate, Greg, Joe, Catherine, Barbara, and John Sr., have all been supportive throughout the process. My son Simon and daughter Macie are still a bit young to read this book, but I hope they will enjoy it when they can. I can't wait to take them out on the trails.

# Introduction

In this era of specialized riding, trail riding sometimes seems yet another closed sport. But it's not so. Trail riding really is for everyone, every day, whether we ride in the city parks or share the open fields with foxhunters.

Trail riding is nothing like riding in a ring or practicing for a particular sport, when patterns are learned and the same rhythms are experienced day in and day out. It is full of variety and surprises, and even the same trail can yield two different experiences on two different days. Trail riding gives us time to connect with the outdoor part of riding and our horses a change from repetition and routine. These days, more and more riders learn at riding stables that have indoor and outdoor arenas, which get used far more than the fields and trails that surround them. Trail riding—or hacking, as it used to be called—has been relegated to a secondary pursuit for many riders who consider what their horses do in the ring to be their real equestrian calling.

Monotony can easily set in for horse and rider when their days are passed looking at the same walls and performing the same moves over and over again. Because trails vary in terrain and scenery, a horse will not get bored and tired the way he may trundling around a ring day after day. Riders will not only find themselves refreshed by trail riding, they will also see a noticeable difference in a formerly ring-sour horse when he gets back to his regular routine.

The difference between a horse who is always kept in a stall and one allowed some turnout is readily apparent. Any horse who has been stall-kept for a while will relish playing in a field with some buddies, eating grass, and generally being a horse. Taking to the trails can be turnout for the rider. While equestrian sports depend on and demand practice and repetition for continued success, the trail offers freedom and ease. It gives the horse's mind a break, and the rider's too.

Even with all its relaxation benefits, the trail can still be a place to train and learn as well. The satisfaction that comes from setting out for a ride on a horse you have brought along to be a sane, sensible, and surefooted trail partner is as great as completing a clean round in the jumper arena. Both achievements come from time and effort invested in worthwhile riding pursuits.

This book is for riders who want to learn how to start trail riding and for trail riders looking for new ideas. It's about appreciating the chance for a long Saturday in the saddle, or even just a quick walk around the farm at sunset. It's about making the most of the time we spend outside with the horses we love.

# Finding and Building
## The Trail Horse

1

**Y**our horse is crucial to having a rewarding trail ride. It doesn't matter if your mount is a retired jumper, an actively competing reiner, or a natural-born trail horse. The good news is that any of these candidates—annded ied, many horses—can be trail partners. With time and seasoning, you can turn just about any horse into an ideal trail companion.

No matter what the terrain, weather, or company, your horse makes the ride a success or failure. Whether you are taking a break from your regular routine or setting out on your daily ride, working with him both while you are riding outdoors and while you are in the ring can make trail time become increasingly enjoyable.

## Looking for a Trail Horse

If you decide to trail ride as your primary equestrian activity, there's no reason not to look for a horse whose main job has been trail riding. He will be used to what you want him to do. Just as you would not necessarily buy a horse trained as a polo pony if you wanted to take up jumping, you may prefer a proven trail horse. He'll be accustomed to varying footing, weather, and sights. If you buy him locally, he may even have been ridden on some of the same trails you're planning to use, which is a benefit since he will be familiar with any sights and obstacles found on those trails.

You can avail yourself of any number of sources in your search for a trail partner, including horse classified ads, bulletin boards, online classified sites, and of course, word of mouth, one of the best ways of all. You may even be able to find a horse for free if you will take a former competitor off the hands of his owner who can no longer provide for him.

Horses heading into retirement are often good trail horses, unless their retirement has been forced by an injury or condition that makes it tough for them to be ridden for any length of time. Even if you do not plan to do much beyond walking and trotting on the trail, it is nice to know that you don't have to curtail the length of your rides because of soundness or fitness issues.

But beware. Often "trail horse" is a synonym for "backyard ornament" to some of the people who are seeking a good home for a former riding partner. If a horse's show career ended because of an injury, he may never be sound enough for any kind of hard work, including long trail rides. But if it ended because he simply got too old for the rigors of competition, or if he had the kind of injury that stops him from being jumped or barrel raced but not from being ridden, you may be in luck. So be sure that you have your trail horse prospect checked as thoroughly by a veterinarian as you would a competition horse. The needs are different, but your desire for a horse that can do what you want him to do is just as strong. The last thing you want is to be left at the barn hand-walking your lame horse while everyone else goes trail riding.

Searching for a trail horse can be easier than looking for a competition partner. For one thing, breeding does not matter a bit for a horse who will be your trail horse. Many people use Quarter Horses and Appaloosas, which have reputations as sturdy animals and solid citizens under saddle. And Arabians, of course, are

famous for their endurance abilities. But any breed or crossbreed of horse can make an excellent trail horse. All horses, including Thoroughbreds, draft horses, ponies, and "Heinz 57" mixes can be suited to life on the trail.

If you want a gaited horse, however, breed becomes important. If you have back problems and have turned to trail riding as a gentler sport than the one you formerly enjoyed, you might consider a gaited horse, such as a Paso Fino, Saddlebred, Icelandic Horse, Rocky Mountain Horse, or Tennessee Walking Horse. Because these horses are bred to move smoothly, their way of going may be easier on a sore back than the jolting walk or trot of some horses. Gaited horses are easy to learn on, which makes them comfortable for novice riders.

Otherwise, the horse's personality matters a lot more than his breed. Even an off-the-track racehorse can be a good trail horse if he's a relaxed and attentive animal. Quiet draft horses and draft crosses are often solid trail mounts, and outgrown children's ponies can contentedly take to the trail with a small adult after

Regardless of size and shape, most horses can make able and willing trail companions.

years of trucking around the ring. Grade, or non-registered, horses can make fine trail partners as well as the most blue-blooded of Thoroughbreds.

If breeding doesn't matter, then what makes a good trail horse? Time and exposure to the trail are two of the most important things, and those you can give your trail horse. For starters, though, a good trail horse is not overly spooky. He is reasonably surefooted, although horses grow more careful the more time you spend riding rough terrain. While soundness is important in any riding horse, it's essential in a trail horse. To have your horse chronically come up lame when you are miles from home is an unpleasant and sometimes dangerous prospect. Not only will you need to walk him back, but also you'll worry that you're doing further damage to him.

A solid trail horse is generally alert and takes in his environment as he works, but doesn't pause every few steps to toss his head, prick his ears, and seem to grow a couple of hands taller. He's in good shape, and he isn't "hot," which is to say he is happy to walk or trot for a few hours without needing a good long canter. But he is also game. It's tough to make a horse who is easily bored or sour into an enjoyable trail partner. It's ideal if your horse has the kind of easygoing and up-for-anything personality that makes him energetic without being flighty, and forward-moving without being too strong.

## Shopping

One of the best ways to find a trail horse is to get the word out that you are looking for a horse. The horse community grapevine grows thick and strong in most riding areas, and there is a good chance that a trainer or rider will hear about horses coming up for sale, and that you are looking to buy. If no one says, "I know the perfect horse for you," then you will have to initiate a search yourself.

You might begin by looking at local newspapers and magazines. Areas with large horse populations typically have publications specifically targeted to horse owners. Advertisements for trucks and horse trailers as well as horses are a feature. Look for these publications at tack and feed stores, and while you are there, check the bulletin board and ask the people behind the counter if they know of any decent trail horses for sale. You never know when someone will have heard of a good candidate. Also, any local horse events, from horse shows to horse auctions, usually post flyers or announcements advertising horses for sale near the venue.

If you choose to do some horse shopping with your computer, the actual process of browsing for horses varies from website to website. Usually, shoppers enter such parameters as breed, location, and price. Some sites even allow preferences like bloodlines, height, color, and discipline to be included. Searches can be customized, and users can specify whether, for example, to include ads without photos or ads for horses who have already been sold. Once choices are entered, the site returns a list of horses with descriptions. At this stage, shoppers open the ads for the horses they find appealing, and browse online for a horse as they would for any other merchandise, reading descriptions, looking at pictures, and considering options.

Looking for a trail horse on classified ad websites and in equine newspapers and magazines can be enjoyable, as it demonstrates how many horses there really are out there. It also gives you a pressure-free way to browse and begin to get a sense of what you are looking for, and what you can expect to find, and what you'll have to pay. You may want to search locally first, unless money is not a limiting factor, as both traveling to look at horses and paying to have them shipped can be expensive.

Here are some terms that you may see in classified ads—in print and online—selling a trail horse:

Trail-Sound Only: Perhaps this horse used to compete, but is now unable to do so due to a physical problem. This can suggest a good prospect, but it can also mean heartbreak. You should always do a vet check.

Companion Horse: It sounds like this horse would be a good buddy, but it actually means he is not rideable. Instead, he would make a good companion for another horse.

Hilltopper: Hilltoppers are riders who follow the hunt but are not part of the formal group, so a horse accustomed to hilltopping will be used to riding out and should do well on the trail.

Ladies' Horse: A gentle horse.

Husband's Horse: The updated version of the "ladies' horse." Now that so many women are the more experienced rider in a couple, the gentle, knockaround horse has become a husband's horse.

Kid-Safe, Novice-Safe, Beginner-Safe, etc.: These all mean the horse is very quiet.

Schoolmaster: Used as a lesson horse, or gentle enough to be used in that way.

Traffic-Safe: Used to being ridden on roads with cars.

A (horse's name.): Sometimes a horse is referred to by his sire's name, so that "This is a nice Native Dancer gelding" means that the horse's sire was the stallion Native Dancer.

Loud, flashy, lots of chrome: These descriptions all refer to a horse with a lot of color. (Chrome is, specifically, white.)

Top side/bottom side: How breeding is recorded. The stallion's information goes on top and the mare's on the bottom. (An ad might read, "Nice, quiet, QH gelding with Peppy San Badger on top and Zip's Chocolate Chip on the bottom." This means that his sire is a son or other direct descendant of the stallion Peppy San Badger, and his dam is a daughter or other direct descendant of Zip's Chocolate Chip.)

Because of their reputations for quiet and sensibility, many people looking for a trail mount turn to Quarter Horses and other breeds commonly used by Western riders. Although Quarter Horses are able English partners, many offered for sale will have been ridden Western. If you don't ride Western yourself, you may not be used to some of the colorful as well as illuminating terms Western riders use to describe horses.

Some of the most common are:

Rides and slides: This horse was trained to be a reining (a sport some consider the Western version of dressage) horse.

Lots of whoa and go: An obedient horse with plenty of energy, if not necessarily calm.

Dead broke: Very well trained and calm.

Foundation: Can trace its bloodline back to the foundation sires of the Quarter Horse breed.

Ranch bred: Hardy, foundation horses bred for work instead of show. They make good, sturdy trail mounts.

Jog, lope: Western terms for trot and canter.

## Long-Distance Shopping

The down side to looking at a "distant" horse (whether you find him online or otherwise) is that you may not be able to see him in the flesh. If a horse who lives far away catches your eye, ask the seller for more photographs than are on the site, and a video. While videos have long been a key part of buying show horses, now even those who are selling broodmares or trail horses often shoot film. Some show the horse being handled as well as being ridden, in order to demonstrate his temperament and his athleticism.

Despite the technological advantages of video and photographs, and long-distance calls to a local vet who knows the horse well, doing without the option of actually meeting the horse before purchase can be difficult. Even if you decide to rule out horses you can't see in the flesh, horse sale sites can still help you by finding what is available in your area. Focusing a search 100 miles—or less—from your home zip code will return nearby horses. As you visit them, you may learn about local farms and horses you would not have encountered otherwise. Of course, the more horse people you know, the more likely someone will spot the very prospect you want, and contact you.

Once you've found the horse you like, you're ready to negotiate a sale. This is where the online experience resembles any other method of horse shopping. Common sense should prevail, even with long-distance transactions. A vet check before you buy is key. That way, you have all the tools to assess the horse's suitability for his job. If you're comfortable with working long-distance, ask a local vet to look at the horse for you if your vet cannot make the trip. Your veterinarian, trainer, or friends may have contacts in the area who can give you the name of a good vet. Experts recommend that every transaction be represented by something in writing to make it legally binding. Even without a lawyer-authored document, it's a good idea to draw up a letter that both parties can agree to and sign.

## The Vet Check

It might be tempting to skip the vet check when you are shopping for a trail horse. Vet checks can be expensive, and when you are excited about getting a new horse the last thing you may want to do is wait for a vet appointment, then wait for test results, then wait to hear about any weaknesses the horse has. You may have gone through all of this for a show horse, but for "just a trail horse," it may seem unnecessary.

Unless you have a vet check, there is no other way to tell if the horse is up to doing what you expect of him. It's best to have your own vet do the exam. If the seller offers to have her vet do it, politely say that you'd prefer yours, as you don't want a conflict of interest. (Her vet, however, may have potentially useful information about the horse's history, and can be a valuable resource.)

A pre-purchase exam should check your potential new horse for soundness and evaluate general health. Make sure you discuss everything that concerns you with your vet during a pre-purchase exam; she will be able to advise you if you're looking at a potential hunt partner or a lawn ornament. Ultimately, a vet check, though expensive, can save you a lot of money if it helps you avoid an unhealthy or unsound horse.

Keep in mind that the veterinarian's check provides an evaluation of the horse only on the day he's being seen. You may also get extra testing, like X-rays or blood work. But don't expect the vet to tell you whether or not to buy the horse, or how much you should pay. Those are decisions you will make on your own with the information you glean from the vet check.

At the exam, the veterinarian will palpate (feel) the horse's body, checking for old injuries and any imperfections. As she feels the horse's legs, she will be checking for healed-over injuries or other unsoundnesses that could affect the horse's way of going. She will examine each foot and hoof for conditions like founder or windpuffs, and for general swelling. She'll flex each joint, and use hoof testers to check each hoof for sensitivity.

She will also want to watch the horse move. Your vet may ask the horse's handler—who can be you or a helper—to spin the horse in a circle so she can see if he appears to have any neurological problems, and to jog him toward and away from her so she can see any lamenesses or irregularities in stride. In a flexion test, the vet flexes the limb to exert pressure on the joint. She then releases and has the handler jog the horse off to see how the joints fare under duress. Many vets will next ask that the horse be ridden so that they can evaluate him for the job he's supposed to do. You may want to ride the horse, or you can ask the seller to do so. It's best to be in a place with various surfaces, so the vet can see how the horse reacts to different footing. She can then evaluate his

The current owner
can tell you all
about the habits
and history of the
horse for sale.

comfort at all his gaits. This bit of exertion from being ridden will enable her to check him for respiratory problems as well.

The vet may recommend a few follow-up tests. If she suspects that the horse is drugged, she may want to do a blood screen. Other conditions become most apparent through other technology, like ultrasound or X-ray. Only you can decide how far to proceed with testing for a trail horse prospect.

The vet check will usually uncover something, because rarely is a horse medically perfect. Then it's up to you to decide if you can live with whatever that something is. If a horse is sound at the vet check, you may decide to live with an old bowed tendon. You may do the same thing if he has arthritis that no longer seems a problem. But be very cautious before purchasing a horse that has foundered or is navicular. These conditions heavily predispose a horse toward lameness and can be harbingers of more costly medical care. If the veterinarian discovers a serious condition, don't assume that because you are buying him just to trail ride that he will be all right. It's still best to steer clear of a horse who may need more time off and medical attention than you are prepared to give.

## At Auction

Auctions can be a fine place to find trail horses, especially since you are not limited to a particular breed. Some auctions are breed specific, however, and you may find yourself at widely varying auctions. Your next trail horse might be found at a Quarter Horse auction that features roping exhibitions, or the dispersal of a Thoroughbred or Standardbred racing stable. Auctions, because they allow you to look at so many horses at once, make horse shopping easier as well as a lot of fun.

Scheduled and reputable auctions offer nice horses of all ages and descriptions. Typically an auction catalog details the horse's breeding, and will have a short blurb about him. Catalogs also give the terms and conditions of the sale, as well as information about bidding increments. If you bid on a horse and win, that horse belongs to you as he leaves the auction ring, so bid with conviction. If the horse does not fetch as much as the consignor had hoped he would, there may be no sale.

If you're just starting out in riding, and unless a very sage and patient trainer or knowledgeable friend can advise you, you probably should not go to an auction intending to buy a horse, because the experience will be overwhelming. Beginners are better off with more time than auctions allow to make a decision about buying, but auctions are a good way for a new rider to educate herself by appraising horses. At an auction she can find out what horse catches her eye, and what her trusted trainer or friend finds conformationally passable. Auctions can be useful even if you're "just looking." As each horse gets sold, most auctiongoers will note his price in their auction catalogs. After you have been to several auctions, you'll get a rough idea of what you can expect to spend for a horse you like.

At some auctions, buyers wear riding clothes so that they can work the horse before bidding, and also watch him under saddle, as if they were trying him in his own paddock. Depending on the size and importance of the auction, more time is allowed. Many reputable auctions provide veterinarians on site to do vet checks. If, for any reason, you don't feel you can trust these vets, you may have to talk your veterinarian into attending the auction with you. The key is to find an auction with a good reputation. A reputable establishment usually advertises well ahead of the sale date, provides printed catalogs, and even has a website advertising the horses that will be for sale. Auctions that have been in business for many years tend to use the same large animal veterinarians' group, which often means these vets have developed a good reputation with local buyers. If you request the sale catalog well ahead of time, you can also arrange with the seller and a veterinarian to meet early at the sale grounds for a vet check, or have a veterinarian examine the horse before the sale. Also, seek out local sellers if possible, so you have some reference point as you shop.

Sadly, some auctions are called "killer sales." Such auctions crop up weekly or monthly, sometimes in various locations, and can feature very troubled or abused horses, although some wonderful horses might be available at these sales. Be wary. You don't want to buy a horse that is unrideable, even for a trail career. If you have a good eye and the money and willingness to nurse a horse back to health, these auctions can yield some good—and heartwarming—results.

Rescue organizations offer another purchase option. Rescue organizations usually require a donation that is as much as the horse would cost. These not-for-profit groups do the legwork of rescuing horses in need, and often can supply a trail horse for someone looking for one. Another advantage is that a reputable rescue group will give you a thorough list of the horse's limitations.

## Identification

When you are horse shopping, you'll find that any registered horse is identifiable through his breed registry if his papers are available, and for some breeds, through his tattoo. Thoroughbreds, for example, are tattooed on their upper lips, and before every race, an identifier certifies that the horse is who his owner and trainer say he is. Some Standardbreds, Appaloosas, Arabians, and Quarter Horses have lip tattoos as well, because these breeds also race. Other registries use photographs to verify horse identity.

Without these breed-oriented identifiers, you may wish to have your horse branded or otherwise marked so that he can always be proven yours. Even if your horse is a grade animal, a freeze brand or other mark can provide proof of ownership. If you live in an area with a large livestock population, you probably have a department of branding at your local agricultural agency. In more urban areas, your veterinarian can help you decide how best to mark your horse.

## Making a Trail Horse of the Horse You Already Have

You may already own the horse who is destined to become your trail horse. Your "new" trail horse may be your old jumper who suffered a torn suspensory ligament, or your dressage horse who is simply getting too old to travel to shows. Or your life may change. I bought my Quarter Horse, Romeo, for hunter-jumper training. Two children later, he is my trail horse. The more time he spends out of the arena, the better and more seasoned he gets, but he would not have been my choice had I been searching for a trail horse in the first place. Yet I enjoy trail riding with him as much as I ever liked working him in the ring.

Even a horse you bought to use for another sport can find new life as a trail horse. In these instances, you have the great advantage of already knowing (and loving) your mount. And if you have "work" for him as a trail horse, so much the better. This way, you can keep a horse you've grown attached to and who has worked for you for a long time, instead of having to sell him. He may have a different job, but he's still employed, and that will make all the difference to him as well as to you.

The downside here is that you do know him so well. You

Trail riding offers a new set of challenges and rewards for horses and riders who have been together for a long time.

know that he hates umbrellas and puddles, that he gets finicky if he is away from his pasture mates for too long, and that he has a nasty trick of bolting for home once he sees the barn. While these are things you might tolerate in a horse rarely used outside of an enclosed ring, you expect a different standard of behavior on the trail. It is not fun to set out for a peaceful trail ride and spend the whole time battling your horse because he wants to run home, or because he balks with each step he takes away from the barn. Instead of fighting him, you will have to retrain him for his new job. Once he gets used to the trail, he will be a partner in relaxation for you. But he will need time.

This may be hard. You may imagine that your horse will be delighted to miss the constant workouts, lessons, and being trailered to horse shows. But he might need some time to get used to the fact that trail riding is the program now. You might be looking forward to a relaxing Saturday trail ride after schooling your new dressage competitor all week. But when you go to get your older horse out of the pasture, he's skittish and the trail ride ends up being a less than ideal afternoon.

Too often, we expect our horses to take naturally to the trail. It seems so easy—can't he just walk along? How hard is that? He walks around in the field all the time. This is, after all, a horse who can jump a line of verticals, change leads, and do leg-yields with no problem. But we have to remember that he was used to that. Horses are very much creatures of habit, and the trail changes each time they go out. This is very different from an arena always set up the same way with the same fence, jumps, and gates.

This principle applies when you ask him to switch jobs. Your horse knows how to go around an arena, run barrels, do shoulders-in, or jump courses. He is good at what he usually does, and there are no surprises. What you work on may differ from day to day, but for the most part, he has the routine down. He knows where the spooky shadow in the corner is. He knows what the farm tractor sounds like, because he hears it rumbling around every day. He knows that the barrels or jumps sometimes get moved around from day to day. But each time he starts out on the trail, from the first step he takes, he does not know what is coming.

In time, your horse will know that the rustling down below is probably a squirrel that may, in fact, jump out. He will know that deer can leap out quickly, wooden bridges make a lot of noise, and

Trail riding can help you prepare for show events like the pairs jumping class in which these riders are competing. The rider on the left has lost a stirrup, but is maintaining her position.

branches will brush his rump, and he will have to walk through a few spiderwebs. Although an obstacle may not be in exactly the same place each time, he will build a repertoire of knowledge from experience. But at the beginning, everything is new.

Also, just because you're using your horse to trail ride does not mean he can't keep up his old job. Even a show horse can enjoy and benefit from the trail. You do not have to make an either/or decision about your horse becoming only your jumper or only your trail horse. He can be both.

Some trainers wonder why people think any horse can become a trail horse, when riders tend to agonize so over whether horses are suited to other sports, like polo or barrel racing. But most horses can learn to become trail horses, even if their original training was otherwise. True, some may never take to it. But unlike a horse who is simply too slow to race, or too sloppy to run barrels, a horse who has never been trail ridden before probably can figure it out. The parameters are just so much wider than they are with other equestrian sports, and particularly if you don't plan to participate in competitive trail riding, there is less at stake. Unless you decide to compete in one of the trail sports like trail trials or competitive trail riding, you are not expecting your trail horse to earn you money or ribbons. You are just out to enjoy a safe ride. And that's a goal most horses can help you meet.

## Trail Gaits

A good trail horse is also comfortable to ride. Most horses are comfortable at the walk, which is the typical gait for much trail riding. But sometimes it's nice to trot and canter when there is room and appropriate footing on the trail, and you may be keeping these gaits up for longer than you would in the ring. It's at these times you want your horse to give you a comfortable rather than a jerky ride. Even as a good trail horse works to find his way along a hilly or rocky trail, he stays reasonably stable and easy to ride.

A horse with a jolting trot or canter tends to make his rider tense. Then the two of them bounce around together, with the rider hurting the horse's back and him slamming the rider's joints.

You can find ways to work around a less-than-smooth horse if you're working toward some athletic pursuits, since he may not need to trot or canter for long, and in a freshly dragged sand riding arena everything is more level and easier to predict. But if you are riding at speed over varying terrain, a horse with an uncomfortable gait may simply worsen as he tries to compensate for the uneven ground. You will both be at a higher risk for injury and falls with the added tension.

Unlike a show horse, a trail horse does not need to be handsome and well-conformed. A trail horse's conformation can be quite a departure from the breed standard. Even the most swaybacked horse can be a good trail horse if he is comfortable carrying a rider, and while windpuffs may look bad on a horse who is supposed to compete in halter classes, they don't matter to a trail horse as long as he can move along consistently without pain. An uncomfortable horse is not a good trail mount, but an ungainly one is fine. Movement faults such as paddling or winging won't hurt a trail horse as long as they don't lead to future lamenesses. So while it may seem that there is an overly long list of preferred qualities, the upside to shopping for a trail horse is that you don't need to worry about (or pay for) his appearance, papers, breeding, or other factors that can traditionally drive up the price of a horse.

## Keeping Your Trail Horse

Trail horses do not necessarily benefit from being kept in stalls. While a competition horse stays cleaner in his stall, which makes him easier to groom for schooling and shows, it's all right for a trail horse's coat to bleach out a bit, or for him to show the nicks and scrapes of herd life, all things that might hinder him in the show ring. If he's only used on the trail, his appearance does not need to be pristine, which means that he may be the perfect candidate for pasture board. Also, many trail horses do not necessarily need rear shoes, and some barns do not allow horses shod behind to pasture board, since rear shoes make it more likely that someone will get hurt by a stray kick when horses, as they will, bicker among themselves. Pasture, or field board, is usually cheaper than stall

board. It's not for the horse who needs a lot of supplements or special food, since most pasture horses simply consume the forage that the field supplies, plus hay, but it is a more natural way to keep a horse, and certainly easier and more economical for the owner.

A good pasture has safe fencing and shade, which can be a run-in shed or just a stand of trees. A shed should be big enough for all the horses in the pasture to go in, or the bossiest ones will keep the others out on windy days. If there is no shed, there should at least be an area with trees that the horses can go to get relief from the sun and wind.

Companionable horses are also important. Some barns keep their turned-out mares and geldings separate to avoid too much strife, but it's not necessary in most cases. You know your horse best, so if you know your gelding is "proud cut" or simply gets studdish at times, mixed turnout is probably not best for him. On the other hand, you will expect your trail horse to be calm and accepting of a wide variety of riding partners, so mixed turnout will provide him with a good way to get used to being ridden in mixed company. Some people even ride very well-trained stallions on the trail with mares and geldings around, but this is a job for an expert rider and an exceptionally calm stud.

Blanketing always presents a problem for pasture-kept horses. Many horses don't need blankets at all, and will benefit from growing a thick, shaggy coat in the winter. And you will be happy when the forecast calls for a wintry mix and you don't have to scurry out to the barn. (You will need to make sure a furry horse cools off after exercise; see Chapter 6 for more on winter riding.) If you do blanket a pasture horse, buy a waterproof-breathable blanket and use it on wet and chilly days. Real cold is less stressful for a horse than severe heat, but if even a thickly coated horse gets wet and cold, he may feel very chilled and start shivering, which can use his energy and eventually lead to undesirable weight loss.

If you do decide to keep your trail horse in a stall, he should have some turnout at least. While some horse people leave their horses in unless they are being ridden, this is not an ideal situation for a trail horse, who needs some liberty each day to keep him even-tempered and used to the outdoors. If he is accustomed to his stall more than he is to trees and grass, the novelty of being outside whenever you go to ride him may make him a bit livelier than is comfortable. Also, he will rely on riding time for all of his exercise, both mental and physical. It's all in what he's used to: a horse who has been in a stall his whole life will probably be fine, but if you bring home a pasture horse, he, like my horse Romeo, may get stressed by being put in a stall.

## Trail Barns

It is great to have your own farm where you can keep your trail horses, particularly if you have out-the-barn-door access to trails and areas to ride. But for many riders, the boarding barn is a necessity. Having a place away from home where you can depend upon your horse being well cared for permits many people to enjoy riding who would have to go without horses if they only had the option of keeping their horses at home.

Happily, boarding barns are terrific places for trail horses and riders. If there are people at the barn who share your interest, you may find yourself with a ready-made group of riding buddies. And since trail riding with at least one other rider is ideal for safety as well as camaraderie, it's convenient to stable your horse at a place that provides you with that company.

When you are looking for a place to board your trail horse, the quality of care is, of course, the most important thing. Examine the other horses living at the barn. Do they seem alert, calm, and healthy? Are their coats shining? Are they in good flesh? What do their feet look like? And look at the facility itself. Is it clean? Do the aisles have any protruding nails or equipment left around? Are the tack rooms secure and neat? Is there evidence of rodent infestation?

Any barn that has many horses on pasture board needs to be particularly attuned to the problem of horse theft, because it is often easier for a thief to lead a horse away from a pasture unnoticed than it is to get a horse out of a stall and barn. Especially if the barn sits next to acres of perfect trail riding land, it may also be a target for thieves who could take a horse and slip off unnoticed into the woods or fields. Look for security measures such as no-trespassing signs, good lighting, and a lock for the front gate after

Having other riders to explore with is one of the advantages of boarding your horse at a barn with other trail horses.

hours. Barn dogs and on-site management provide additional security, and some barns even install security cameras to deter thieves of horses and gear.

An understanding barn manager is key to any boarding situation, as well. Sometimes the lone trail rider at a show barn will suffer from the reverse of squeaky wheel syndrome. Since a trail horse is less likely to need the kind of supplements and blanketing that a show animal might, he might get overlooked. But at a trail barn, or any well-managed barn, a trail horse will get the same attention as his barn mates. A good trail horse manager will be particularly attuned to problems such as overwork, soreness, and lameness as well as the usual equine concerns of feeding, bedding, and exercise.

If you plan to trail ride as your primary activity, whether or not the barn has a ring—especially an indoor arena—may not be that important. If you want to save money, you might choose a place without an arena at all. A boarding facility that has good pastureland and trail access could be a perfect place for your horse. Being near or next to a park is a real advantage for a trail barn, but can often drive up board bills. Hacking a little ways over to pick up

Access to local bridle paths from your barn makes trail riding more convenient.

a trail can save some money every month while not fundamentally altering your boarding experience.

Another nice feature for a trail rider is a boarding barn that itself has plenty of land. On quieter days, you may just feel like a walk around the barn, and it is a real luxury, especially in the suburbs, if your spot is large enough to allow you to do that. If your boarding barn has a hay field, ask the manager to consider mowing a perimeter trail that can offer more space for riding. There is something lovely about riding in a hay field, smelling the hay and watching it wave in the wind, without damaging the food your horse is depending upon for the winter or wading through ticks.

## Managing the "Trail-Sound" Horse

If you have bought a horse who was sold as "trail-sound only" you may be in for a lesson in chronic pain management. This route can yield a well-bred and well-mannered horse for a small price, but he may have problems you will have to address so you can ride often and without hurting him. A thorough veterinary exam will tell you whether the horse can be a trail partner for you, and your vet will continue to be an important part of your management plan. Don't completely disregard a horse who has chronic pain. Even a horse who has mildly foundered can go for trail rides, particularly if he has corrective shoeing. If you don't ride too much or too hard, he may be the perfect horse for you.

Unless his previous owner was extraordinarily forthcoming about his condition and how she managed it, you will probably have to experiment with pain therapies. Often these don't involve drugs. Arthritic horses, for example, can stay useful if they are kept warm and moving gently. For these animals, short sessions of riding and turnout may work best. Corrective shoeing may help a navicular horse who seems "ouchy" often, as can keeping him off pavement and gravel. Phenylbutazone (commonly called "bute") can provide occasional relief.

Don't disregard alternative therapies for your trail horse. Some people swear by acupuncture, and you can also have a

massage therapist or chiropractor work on your horse. These chiropractors subscribe to the idea that joint problems can affect neurological balance. With manual adjustments, they help horses to feel better under saddle as well as out in the field. If your horse's lameness or soreness can't be pinpointed by your veterinarian, chiropractic therapy may help. Be sure that the chiropractor you select is educated and certified by a local licensing board.

Grass is easier on a horse's feet than riding on hard pavement or rocky roads.

Horses improve
their training on
the trail just as
they do in the ring.

# **Riding** the Trail Horse

## 2

Once you have your trail horse, it is time to mount up and start enjoying him. Whatever type of riding training you have under your belt already will serve you well on the trail, from hunter-jumper to dressage. The same goals of attention, collection, and work apply to the trail just as they do in the ring. As easygoing an activity as trail riding is, your horse is still better off when he is concentrating on his job. It's no better for a trail horse to poke along and stumble than it is for a jumper to do so. The trail is an excellent place for your horse to relax and for you to take a break, but he also needs to engage himself.

The special concerns of the trail are mostly dealing with spooking and how to handle all the different sights and sounds you and your horse will encounter each time you set out. Even a seasoned show horse, used to crowds and noise, will need some time to get accustomed to deer and off-leash dogs. (How to handle various terrains, like hills and streams, is covered in Chapter 6.)

# Spooking

Spooking—or shying—is what a horse does when something alarms him. Many horses jump sideways when they spook. Some rear, or even bolt away. Horses spook because they perceive things so differently from us—what looks like a trash can with a squirrel in it to you and me seems to be a horse-gnawing monster to your horse. Physically, horses are very sensitive, with cupped ears that magnify sound and even detect some ultrasonic vibrations. Their skin ripples if they feel a fly, and their sense of smell is also sensitive—just try putting medicine in your horse's feed one day. While their vision is not as good, they can see all the way around because of how their eyes are set. Objects in their peripheral vision, however, will often be blurry and seem more threatening than those right in front of them.

What makes horses spook varies as widely as horses themselves, but the following things make many horses spook: trash blowing along the ground, odd sounds (glass breaking, a new car starting), really loud sounds (car backfiring), sudden movements (someone jumping out, another horse galloping), anything that flaps in the wind (horse blanket drying on a fence), anything moving overhead (wind through branches, you taking off your jacket). Because of all the unpredictable things that can happen outside the controlled environment of the arena, spooking and the resulting accidents from bolting or throwing the rider are major concerns for trail riders.

Besides being safer, a horse who tends not to spook—the "desensitized" horse—makes trail riding more pleasant. If your horse has a tendency to bolt after he spooks, you may feel some trepidation about heading out on the trail, where the unexpected happens all the time. Should a groundhog rustle, you don't want that to prompt your horse to shy and run for home. Even if you get him calmed down, a noisy shower of acorns might bother him. Next, some deer could dart across your path, and then a cyclist could call out from behind you that he wants to pass. If your horse is skittish, any of these things can seriously unhinge him. He may shy and bolt, and you could fall off. Even if you are an experienced rider who seldom gets unseated from a spook, it's an experience best avoided.

The fear of your horse spooking can well make your more ride less enjoyable. If you constantly wonder what will cause him to spook, most likely you'll sit deeper and clutch the reins. He may respond to your cues more than a noisy truck, for example, and think that something scary is going on simply because of how you're acting. Then the two of you are locked in an unpleasant and non-productive cycle. Neither of you can relax and each is jittery, wondering what the other will do next.

Even if you conquer your own fears and can relax as you ride, your horse will still shy once in a while. There is no such thing as a horse who never spooks. Even police horses, world-renowned for their level-headedness and ability to walk through crowds and parades, spook sometimes. But getting your horse to a point where spooks are reduced to rare occurrences or limited to a jump sideways instead of bolting will benefit both of you. And you will learn to ride him when he shies. Well-balanced and experienced riders don't come off or allow their day to be ruined just because their horse spooks; they gather him back up and move on.

An important part of accomplishing this goal is recognizing the signs that your horse may spook. Some spooks come on very fast, without warning. But some horses will plant their legs in front

This horse's alert expression and pricked ears demonstrate that he is attuned to some environmental stimulus.

of them, throw their heads up, or otherwise demonstrate that they are frightened and may be trying to activate the "flight" portion of their herd animal's fight-or-flight instinct. As you get to know your horse better and better, you'll learn his signals as well as what is liable to bother him. Some horses hate dogs, and others dislike harsh shadows. (In fact, it's not uncommon for a horse to be "afraid of his own shadow." It is nothing to be ashamed of.) If you hear dogs barking and think they may be unleashed, there's no reason for you not to hop off if you think your horse may react dangerously. (See Chapter 4 for more on sharing the trail.)

Rider fear is a legitimate part of trail riding. If your vision of trail riding is still restricted to horses-for-hire who are used to the exact same trail every day, then it seems ridiculous to be scared. But trail riding can magnify rider fear or anxiety if the rider's horse does become spookier outside the arena. Concentration and mental focus can alleviate these fears; however, simply forcing yourself to ride through the fear without working on it may just make you more scared and eventually lead to a truly scary situation, like a runaway horse. If you feel trepidation about trail riding, start off slowly with short rides, take it easy by choosing your days, trails, and companions carefully, and your confidence will increase with each successful ride. Just as someone rattled by jumping too high would start with cavaletti and crossrails again, an unnerved trail rider can start with a walk with a friend around the pasture, then on the trail, then the pasture alone, and so on, until he is back to riding alone on the trail. A runaway horse may still alarm you, but that won't keep you from climbing on again for another ride.

## Cows

Cows—or "cattle" as Western riders prefer to call them—are part of riding out. A herd of Holsteins peacefully grazing is one of the bucolic scenes a rider hopes to see while riding through farmland. Nothing seems more natural than watching a well-trained cow horse move through a herd of cows. But to horses unused to them, cows are scary. Between their loud coloring, their horns, and their mooing, cows have many horse-frightening attributes. As with anything else, time and experience can turn a skittish trail horse into a cow pony.

When the cows are grazing or resting is a good time to try to ride by. Ride your horse up and down the fence until he relaxes. He will probably keep an eye and ear on the cows, but if you make your trip seem mundane, he will take his cue from you. Calves in particular may scare your horse, as they will run zigzagging up to the fence and say hello. Your horse may spook and snort at this wild sight, but will eventually realize that the fence is separating him from the calf and may relax then.

Riding on a range or in any area where cattle are allowed to roam (which could be your neighbor's pasture), you may encounter cows who are not confined. Only experience can make a horse used to this. If you can, stay mounted. Remember that cows can shy and spook just like horses, and you don't want to get them going. Keep your voice down for the same reason. Then watch your footing so that if your horse bolts, you're all right, and take a deep seat.

Cows will usually be sprawled across their pasture in the morning and the evening, when they like to graze. When it gets hot at midday, they will sleep in the shade, and tend to group up more. Anywhere there is water, too, cows will gather. So if you're riding along a creek, you may run into a group of cows. The best way to ride through situations like this is with someone on a hackneyed cow pony, who can convince your horse with his calm that cows are nothing to fear. If you're alone with a horse who is not used to cows, avoid large groups of them, even if they are all hunkered down for a nap. You never know when one will shy at your horse, and then things can heat up quickly.

## Cars and Road Riding

Cars and horses do not mix. Pavement is just not made for horses, despite what city carriage horses need to do every day. Keep your horse to a walk when you have to ride on a road. The surface is too hard for horses, and it's slippery, too. It can make your horse sore and more likely to fall if you ride fast. Cars, for their part, make unpredictable noises that scare horses, and they pose a significant threat to horses who can be injured or killed by them if they get loose or something else happens to create an accident-ready situation. If you ride in a suburban area, though, cars are part of your riding life.

The best way to keep yourself and your horse safe when riding around traffic is through exposure and training. A horse who is accustomed to the sights and sounds of cars, and can be relied upon to listen when you ask him to stop or go, is already ahead of the game. We have all seen police horses sashay through traffic without a care in the world. While your horse may never reach that level of nonchalance—and he does not need to—with time and effort, he can learn to be ridden in an area also used by cars and trucks. If you don't have a trailer, riding on the road may be the only way you can get out. So getting along with cars becomes a crucial way of life.

Because the stakes are so high when it comes to car and horse safety, practice with your horse on a quiet road with occasional cars until he becomes used to the idea of riding near them. If your horse is turned out alongside a road, he will be significantly less troubled by backfiring and horns when you are riding, because it's nothing new to him. But a horse who lives in a quiet pasture or stable will need some time to sort things out the first times he realizes he is expected to coexist with these noisy and smelly monsters.

You should cross roads at a walk since pavement is so difficult for horses to navigate. Horses can easily slip on asphalt if they move too fast, and many of them don't like the sounds their hooves make as they cross, so they will start high-stepping as soon as their feet hit the unfamiliarly hard surface.

Before crossing a road, look carefully at the situation to evaluate the best crossing point. You want to be visible to oncoming traffic, so, just as you were taught as a child, look both ways before attempting to cross. If you are near a "blind" curve or other tricky spot, it might be best to walk along the road for a while until you find a more suitable place to cross. Alternatively, cross diagonally. Even though you'll be in the road for a longer time, you will still be more apparent to drivers as you go, which is ultimately safer.

If you're riding in a group, one rider may choose to ride into

the middle of the road and dismount, then hold up a hand like a traffic cop to allow the other riders to go behind her. On a straightaway, everyone can cross at one time, so that things move along more swiftly for the cars. The whole group should wait to move until the last rider has finished crossing.

When you are riding alongside a road, hug the shoulder away from traffic as tightly as you can. If a car making an unusual noise is coming up behind you, allow your horse to face it if possible. Sometimes out-of-the-ordinary vehicles like a logging truck with pennants attached to the back logs, or a big trailer, will startle horses more than the usual cars and trucks. If you don't have room to turn him all the way around, at least let him turn his head to see what's coming. Sometimes that helps him settle down and realize a familiar object is approaching.

Part of what draws people to live in semi-rural areas is often the vision of riders out for the day, walking along a country lane. So even non-horsey people are usually delighted to see riders out on a road, and will oblige you if you ask them to stop or slow down for you. You may have to stand while a mother points your

Riders crossing a road carefully, keeping their horses at a walk. For maximum safety, the leader should keep both feet in the stirrups.

horse out to her children, but in general, suburban dwellers seem happy to accommodate riders. They just have to know you are there, so mount a public relations campaign through posters, flyers, and even pony rides or bake sales to keep your neighborhood aware that there are horses on the road. Signs at frequent horse crossings also help keep people understanding that they need to share the road with equestrians. The more aware drivers are of local riders, the better for both parties.

Local laws usually ask riders to stay on the right side, which usually works fine. But when riders are faced with a road that dives rightward, or a hill that prevents them from seeing if cars are coming, it can be tough to heed that law. These may be good times to lead your horse, or to ride on the left side of the road for a moment. When you have to lead your horse alongside a road, lead him along the right shoulder, with him to your right.

Railroad crossings, too, are sometimes inevitable on horseback. If you need to cross tracks often, make an effort to find out the train schedule so that you can avoid busy times.

## Dogs

Horses and dogs just naturally seem to go together. Horse people love their dogs—from Jack Russells to Corgis, Blue Heelers to Foxhounds. Foxhunters depend upon their hounds (never "dogs") as a crucial part of their sport, which consists of riders chasing their prey with a whole pack of canine companions.

Dogs do, however, often cause some trouble for trail riders. It seems counterintuitive that a little yapping dog might startle a horse one hundred times his weight, but it happens all the time. Also, bridle paths are perfect places to walk dogs for many people, even if they are not supposed to be on them. Because so many more people have dogs than horses, it seems that dog walkers take to the bridle paths with impunity, and can sometimes even act surprised to see you. Many people are ignorant about horses, and have no idea how threatening a dog can seem to a horse. Off-leash dogs in particular bother horses because they come barking up and sometimes even threaten to nip. It is perfectly acceptable to ask the

Many horses don't mind dogs, but exercise caution especially when dogs are off-leash.

owner to put the dog back on the leash, even though the owner may not be thrilled about it.

Remember that avoiding confrontation between the two animals is not just about the dog bothering your horse. Your horse could hurt the dog, too. If the dog surprises him and nips, your horse could wheel and kick, and if he connects, he could injure or kill the dog. Groups of dogs particularly alarm horses, by tending to whip themselves up. (Because experienced fox-hunting horses are used to hounds, they make good trail horses; they learned to wade through gangs of moiling dogs without giving it a second thought.)

Even without barking, off-leash dogs seem to find ways to spook horses by the way they rustle through leaves or dart out from behind rocks. So many barns have resident dogs that your horse may be used to them, but each new one presents a new situation. Exposure will help, and being polite but clear with owners is another good way to reduce possible stress and danger.

Your own dog may be used to your horses, and the horses in turn used to your dog. If he often accompanies you on rides around the farm, you are all used to having him at your heels, sniffing as he goes. But when you are riding in a park or on other trails, it's best to leave him at home, no matter how heartbroken he looks when you set off. You simply can't keep a responsible eye on him while you're riding, and even though he knows your horse well, he may antagonize other horses or dogs he meets. Since you can't very well keep him on a leash on horseback, he's better off left behind.

## Desensitizing Work at Home

The word "bombproof" describes a horse who is so quiet and sensible that even if a bomb went off, he would not spook or bolt. There are many ways to make your horse fit this description through becoming more confident on the trail. As you begin his education, you may actually be starting from experience. Perhaps you already had one less-than-fun ride where your horse took off when he saw a bicycle. Now you know you have to deal with bicycles.

You may be able to do some desensitizing at the moment you see a potential spooking event. For instance, when you see a cyclist coming toward you, say hello. This may encourage the cyclist to say hello to you in return. His greeting will inform your horse that the cyclist is a person, just like you, instead of a shiny monster with wheels. But the cyclist may race by, sunshine glinting off his machine, helmet obscuring his face, and scare your horse.

Once you are home, you can handle your horse's fears in your own time and at your own pace. To help him conquer a fear of bikes, for example, you'll need a buddy and a bicycle. In the confines of the arena, lean the bike up against the rail. Lead your horse in (no need to be riding during this), and let him smell it. If he doesn't want to go near it, just stand with him wherever he is comfortable. This may take time. Ideally, you want him to approach the bike on his own. Horses, being the curious creatures that they are, will probably want to investigate eventually. But don't rush him, or you may wind up in the same thrashing or bolting predicament that brought you to a riding ring with a horse and a bicycle in the first place.

After your horse has sniffed the bicycle, have your buddy move it around a little bit. Let the horse see the metal gleam and hear the noises that it makes. He may shy again. Stay patient,

With time and training, horses can become accustomed even to speeding bicycles.

letting him decide when to approach and check it out. Again, it may be a while. (This may be your only activity for the day.) Eventually, it would be nice if he relaxed enough around the bicycle for your friend to hop on and pedal around him. This will simulate the noise he heard and the experience of this unfamiliar machine coming up behind him. Your horse may never get to the point of ignoring bicycles. He may always stop when he hears one. But if you can desensitize him to its presence and noise enough so that he doesn't shy at them, then you can stop worrying about bikes every time you go trail riding. And there is no need for him to love bicycles; he just has to get bored enough that he will walk by one without being startled, and allow one to come up behind him, too.

Many spooky objects that you may encounter on the trail can be handled this way. Depending upon how serious the problem is, and how enterprising you are feeling, you can gather items like baby strollers and backpacks, and even dogs, to help your horse adjust within the safety of a familiar ring or paddock. There is always the chance that something unusual, like the odd recumbent bike or baby-in-a-backpack, will throw you a curve, but for the most part, once horses get over what has scared them, they remember and adjust. On the other hand, what looks the same to you may look different to him at another time. So a baby stroller casting a strong shadow on a sunny day may seem like a different object than the hooded one you encountered in the drizzle a week ago. You cannot possibly prepare for every eventuality, but constant exposure to new sights and sounds can only help your horse become more accustomed to the world around him and help you be more confident as you ride.

Changing your horse's living situation may also help him on the trail. If cars are primarily what spook your horse, you may be able to make him calmer by changing where he is turned out. If he usually grazes in a quiet, out-of-the-way pasture, see if there is a spot closer to a road that might work. Then more cars will go by, and he may get used to the noises during turnout instead of when you are on his back. When you first turn him out, he may be skittish from the change in scenery as well as from the cars going by. But as the afternoon wears on, and he hears sirens, horns, and brakes squealing, he may become inured to the sounds. Then, the next time you are riding and there is an automotive racket, he'll be dealing with a known quantity instead of something he interprets as dangerous.

For a horse frightened by deer or other woodland animals, the reverse can work. Such a horse may benefit from being moved from a traffic-fronting pasture to one adjoining woods or a quieter field where deer are likely to congregate. Because of the sudden way that they bound out of bushes, and the flashes of white in their tails, deer seem especially likely to scare horses. Also, where there is one deer, several are sure to follow. It is very alarming to be riding along a quiet forest path and have a deer sprint out of a copse. But as with cars, if the horse gets used to the startling movements of deer while he is grazing, he will eventually stop reacting to them on the trail. He may never ignore them entirely, but he may grow accustomed to the rustling and the accompanying burst of action that deer provide. Many horses will pause and prick their ears when they see a deer or sense that one is nearby. The idea is to keep it at that, and then be able to ask that your horse move on, at least until the next deer shows up. His job is to listen to you, not to worry about the deer, so you need to keep his mind on you.

Beware of desensitizing quick fixes. There are audio tapes available that promise to desensitize your horse. They contain noises like truck horns and thunder, and the idea is that you play these noises so much for your horse that he will be accustomed to them the next time he hears them. That may happen. But it is more likely that the situation will be different enough to cause him to spook. Thunder across an open field accompanied by lightning, for example, will be different from hearing taped thunder in the safety of the barn.

## Desensitizing on the Trail

Other horses can help you desensitize your horse. If he will accept being the horse in the rear on a trail ride, having a more experienced horse in front of him will show him that there is nothing to fear. Your horse may be eyeing a wooden bridge up ahead suspiciously, and may even startle at the sound that the lead horse's hooves make when they clatter on the wood. But if he sees his buddy calmly walk over the obstacle, he will be far more likely to take it himself without complaining, or at least follow eventually.

Many horses
find machinery
intimidating, but
with a little time
and patience
will become
used to it.

If you have a friend with a more experienced horse, so much the better. And if the more experienced horse belongs to you, enlist someone to ride him while you school the new guy. The two of you can head out for a real training ride. If you're really not sure how your horse is going to react to everyday trail obstacles, it's polite to consider the other people in the group and leave him until he is more reliable. Otherwise, everyone may be held up while you try to convince your horse that each pile of leaves is not a brown and crunchy monster. Try to make a point of taking your horse out with a campaigner, and let his owner know that you're using her horse as a model. (And then take her out to lunch for doing you the favor of waiting for eons while your horse considers whether to move on down the trail or not.)

Take heed, however, that the reverse is often true. Horses who see other horses react to something often decide that it is more serious than they initially thought. That's why it's best for the calmer horse to be in the lead. If a log frightens the horse in front, the next one may think twice before stepping over it. But if the first horse casually marches over it as if nothing's there, the horse in back is more likely to do the same.

If your horse is edgy about going through streams or creeks, or even walking over logs, help him out by grabbing some mane in case he does decide to jump across at the last second. You'll be prepared, and you also will not grab him in the mouth, which would teach him never to cross another stream or step over another log.

Remember, too, that you can always get off and walk. You may feel a little silly doing this. After all, you did not saddle up and go out on horseback so you could go hiking while dragging a horse behind you. But if you get scared, it is a lot better to walk along next to your horse than to keep riding through tension and anxiety. Your horse feels both of these keenly, and will probably spook again if he thinks that's what you're expecting. If he did spook, you're expecting it for good reason, and may not be able to relax. In this case, it is better just to walk. Walking will relax you, both because of the exercise and because you're giving yourself a break from riding, and your horse will feel less stressed with you on the ground. Next time you will ride.

If your horse spooks at something while you are walking along, just try to hold on to the reins and speak to him calmly. Explain what he saw. He may not understand your words, but he will understand what you're trying to convey. "Those squirrels do seem to come out of nowhere, but they're just squirrels. They won't hurt you. You're a great big horse." Even nonsense is all right, just as long as your voice is soft and reassuring. Remount as soon as you feel comfortable so that things can then proceed as normally as possible.

Another technique for dealing with a horse who appears to be about to spook—walking with his head flung up, taking prancing steps, and generally acting edgy—is to get his head down. It's harder for him to startle and bolt if he has his head down, and it also gives him something else to concentrate on besides what might be around the next corner. One way to do this is by getting your horse on the bit. If getting on the bit is not yet part of your equitation repertoire, just concentrate on gently getting that head down. An approximation of getting your horse on the bit is to keep your reins rather long, hold your hands a bit farther apart than you normally would (not likely to win you any equitation awards) and play gently with the reins, keeping a feel of his mouth, and ask your horse to lower his head. When he is thinking about what you're asking instead of every little thing around him, he is less likely to spook. Sometimes asking for the trot has the same effect, since your horse has to keep his mind on what he is doing more than if he is just poking along waiting to find something to be scared of around the bend.

Choose your days carefully for desensitizing tactics, especially out on the trail. Let's say you've decided that it's time for your horse to get over his fear of wooden bridges. You know exactly the trail you want to ride, you have your bridge picked out, and have worked your schedule to allow yourself plenty of time to ride and to lead him back and forth if you need to. But as you're driving to the barn, you watch through your windshield as branches toss back and forth in a strong wind. It's a sunny, cold, brilliant day so you see the shadows playing on the side of the road. It feels crisp and beautiful and like an excellent day for a hike, but it is not necessarily the ideal time for a trail ride, especially on a horse who is a little dubious about the prospect of trail riding in the first place.

Between the harsh shadows playing around his feet and the leaves and grass blowing against him, your horse may already be a little "up" by the time you get to the bridge. Although it will ruin your plans for the day, you may find it easier to switch tacks. Consider changing your plans and ride on a shady trail, one without as many shadows and with a bit of a wind break. You have to be a little flexible when it comes to desensitizing, because you don't want to trade the fear you're striving to overcome for a new one. It is not particularly helpful to have a horse who does not like to cross bridges become doubly scared that something will blow onto him as he tries to cross.

Seek help with desensitizing your horse if you can. If there are mounted police or rangers in your area, they may be able to help you and other riding friends with some desensitizing techniques. Some offer clinics or classes to help you mimic their training techniques. Law enforcement groups have some of the best-trained and dauntless horses who go through rigorous selection and training in order to be calm around crowds, sirens, and city streets. You can ask one of them to give a demonstration at your barn, or simply ask for tips. Mounted park and city police officers can pass along tips they have learned from dealing with all the things that can upset their horses.

The same applies to parade groups and people who take part in mounted historical reenactments. Their horses are used to being ridden in parades or "battles" that involve loud noises and a variety of onlookers and vehicles. Such horses need to be calm and sane. People who have worked as outriders or riding lead ponies at a racetrack also know a lot about calm horses, because their mounts need to be so steady that they can calm down a fractious racehorse on his way to the starting gate. Someone with experience in these pursuits may be able to help you handle horses in challenging situations as well.

## Ring Work That Helps on the Trail

Besides doing desensitizing exercises, there are other ways to help your trail work while you're in the ring. You can become more skilled at mounting and leading as well as improving your horse's ability to go over obstacles, all while in your enclosed arena.

Ideally, a trail horse should be very easy to mount, as you never know when you are going to have to climb off, whether it's to move a fallen branch or open a gate. Your horse is accustomed to you mounting and dismounting from the left, but a trail horse should allow you to use either side, as you never know which side will be the most convenient for you. Most horses will let you mount easily, but many also like to start walking while you're still trying to get on, which means that you hop along until you can get up, or, more dangerously, your foot gets caught and you get dragged. (More on safety stirrups, which help alleviate this problem, in Chapter 8.)

If you're used to riding in a ring, you may be used to mounting with the help of a mounting block. This is actually better for you, the saddle, and the horse, since it causes less stress on you, your horse's back, and your equipment. But if you're out

on the trail, you cannot always depend upon help to get up. Look for stumps or gates to give you a boost. Other good places for shorter riders (like me) to mount include hay bales, trunk bumpers, or the side of a ditch, with your horse standing in the lowest part. Or ask one of your buddies to give you a leg up. You can also buy gadgets that mimic a cupped pair of hands and use stirrup leather extenders. An old barn trick that mimics extenders is simply to lower your stirrup far below where you would usually position it, then ratchet it back up again once you're on. (It's a tedious process, but effective.)

In order to be self-sufficient on the trail, you need to be able to get on by yourself. This means you need to be limber enough to swing your left leg into the stirrup, and strong enough to push off with your right leg and swing over without hitting your horse in the back. All of this only works if your horse will stand still for it, so practice at home until the two of you can perform your respective parts easily.

When you're riding in a busy area, you are more likely to be on and off your horse several times as you cross roads and open and close gates. Mounting quickly becomes very helpful as you make your way through the landscape. While it often takes many riders a few tries to get enough lift to mount safely, it's best if you can get it done with just one one-footed jump. This way, your horse is less likely to move off without you

To mount quickly, take both your reins in your left hand, maintaining some contact. Place that hand on his withers, but resist the urge to grab mane and haul yourself up. Your left foot goes in the stirrup and your other hand goes on the back of the saddle. Bend your right knee and give one good bounce. Your left foot helps by pressing down. Swing your leg over, and settle down lightly without hurting his back. Get those reins ready and off you go.

If your horse truly does not want to stand still for you, consider that you may be hitting him in the back or jerking him in the mouth as you get on. You may be doing these things without realizing it, so look into your mounting habits first by having someone watch you and see if your horse is responding directly to pressure in either of those spots.

Once you have ruled out potential pain, you can try mounting and dismounting repeatedly, praising your horse as soon as he stands still. Part of the praise is stopping getting off and on. You can also have someone hold the horse's head as you mount. Over time the holder can do less and less holding, and the horse will become used to standing. Repetition in doing it correctly makes the most sense.

Your horse should also know how to stand still when you're

on the trail. You may need to consult a map, get a drink of water, or simply admire the view. Many horses—especially those who have not had the experience of standing in the middle of the ring waiting for judging at a show—get restless once they get moving and will not want to whoa for more than a minute. Ring work can help with this, too. Like holding still while mounting, holding still under saddle takes repetition.

Ask your horse to halt, and then let the reins loose. If he moves off, ask him to halt again. Wait for an uncomfortably long time, until he starts shifting around and you wish you could move off yourself. When he tries to walk again, halt him. Eventually he will get the idea that he needs to wait for you to ask him to move. Work over several sessions until he will stand for longer and longer periods of time and on a looser and looser rein. You should be able to sit and relax without holding him back, and he should stand patiently, waiting for you to decide that it is time to walk on.

You will find it useful if your trail horse will "ground-tie." This means that he stands still when you are dismounted, as if he were tied to the ground. (You should, of course, carry a halter and lead rope with you so that you can actually tie him when you find a hitching post or picket line.) But for those moments when you need to move a branch out of the way, it's more convenient to have him stand still instead of you having to loop the reins over your arm.

You can work on any of these skills on the trail. Practice standing still while a friend opens a gate. If you dismount for any reason, take a few minutes to practice ground-tying before you get back on. All of these skills build on experience and repetition, so they can be easily worked on in the ring as well. But out on the trail is where you will use them, so out on the trail is a good place to practice.

## Tripping

Surefootedness is prized in a trail horse for good reason. When you ride on varying footing and terrain, you need your horse to stay upright and you rely on him to pick his way deftly through challenging areas. If your horse trips often and his problem seems to be getting worse over time, rule out physical causes like foot pain or a neurological disease with a veterinary appointment. One of the most common causes of a horse's tripping is being "long in the toe," meaning overdue for an appointment with the farrier. Fatter horses trip more, and so do tired ones. You'll notice that your horse starts stumbling toward the end of a trail ride when he is fatigued and not as attentive to where he places his feet.

If your horse has conformation flaws, he may trip more often. A horse who is built downhill tends to walk heavily on his forehand (like mine), and has trouble keeping himself balanced enough to avoid tripping. As you ride a horse who is heavy on the forehand, concentrate on helping him learn how to use his "rear engine," and travel with his hindquarters propelling you and his back rounded. Conformation-based issues can be helped by time and training. Avoid martingales or tie-downs on horses who are tripping, since the last thing they need is any hindrance in their motion.

Work in the ring can help your horse trip less. Concentrate on speeding up and slowing down at the walk and trot, and asking for many changes in direction and gait. Work over cavaletti is always a good idea for the stumbling horse since it keeps him thinking about his feet. Anything that helps a horse use his "rear engine" rather than keeping his weight on the forehand will help him be less likely to trip. If he keeps tripping and you just can't figure out why, check that shoeing schedule.

## Riding with a Child: Ponying

Many people turn to trail riding as a perfect family activity. Riders may be at various levels of ability, but everyone can enjoy a trail ride even if one parent is competing at second level dressage, the child has just started lessons, and the other parent only rides on these family outings. Riding with children can be difficult, however. You want them to have a good time, but you also want them to be safe. Children can be very good riders because their reflexes are fast and they have little fear, but this can also make them hazardous to themselves and others.

When starting to trail ride with your child, you may want to pony his horse. (Ponying—sometimes called "snubbing up"—is the act of leading one mounted horse while riding another. You've seen this at the racetrack countless times. It's why even the tallest horse at the track, if his job is to accompany a racehorse to the gate, is called a "pony.") Many horses do this easily, but it is a learned skill just like changing leads on command.

Ponying gives you a measure of control over the horse your young or inexperienced child is riding. The trail provides enough uncertainty, which is why you may want to pony his horse the first few times out. To do this, your horse must be very agreeable and quiet, since the lead rope may drag on the ground or get caught. Also, the other horse may try to nip at him, or lay his head across you and your horse, which are all annoying habits that your horse needs to be able to ignore.

The idea in ponying is not to drag the led horse behind you, but to have the two horses moving similarly. Keep the lead rope in your hand, but don't wrap it around your hand or your saddle horn, since you want to have control and be able to let go if you need to at any time. If the led horse keeps bumping into your horse, or tries to lie across you, make sharp turns to disrupt his activity. If you have reservations about the led horse, keep him on a long enough rope so that if he should rear back, his front feet will not hit your horse.

To get your child's horse used to being ponied, work him on a lungeline. Letting the lungeline trail behind him periodically will get him used to the idea and safeguard you when ponying should you ever need to drop the lead rope.

## Trail Gaits

The walk and the trot are really the best gaits for the trail, because they invite you to look at the scenery around you and enjoy the day as well as work your horse. If your horse is the type who likes to go on the buckle, you may enjoy a calm amble through the woods. Many horses and riders enjoy a slightly more energetic walk, which gives the horse a bit more of a workout but also keeps

him focused on his job of listening to the rider instead of thinking about each leaf on every tree, or getting lazy and stumbling.

A ground-covering walk is an ideal gait for trail riding.

The sitting trot or extended trot you may use in the arena can each come in handy on the trail if you are trying to slow down or make time, but a middling speed or working trot is the best way to cover ground and keep your horse from getting too winded. An overly slow trot or jog invites tripping on roots or other trail obstacles, while a speedy one may not be effective either. Unless your horse is really balanced, he may find it hard to keep his footing once he starts stepping out. Keeping to a steady trot is best, because your horse can breathe comfortably while moving at a reasonable pace.

# 3

# Trail Riding for the Competition Horse and Competing for the Trail Horse

For many riders, trail riding is not their sole sport. In fact, if asked to define themselves, the first response of many people who enjoy trail riding would be that they do dressage or ride jumpers. But even when trail riding is not your sole equestrian activity, it can benefit a competition horse by giving him a mental break from his daily routine while continuing his physical work. Dressage horses, for example, can shoulder-in down the trail as well as in the arena, and the finesse and control required to open a gate or pick through rocks can serve them well in the show ring. Western Pleasure horses can use trail time as a way to practice their traditionally smooth way of going, jumpers can take natural obstacles on the trail instead of only man-made jumps, and endurance riding is, of course, built on a foundation of trail riding.

For anyone who has truly fallen in love with trail riding itself, but likes the idea of competing as well, there are trail sports. Endurance riding and its cousin, competitive trail riding, are probably the most popular. Sports like competitive mounted orienteering and Ride and Tie, which are less commonly pursued, also give trail riders a way to make their hobby an athletic endeavor. Many organizations now offer trail classes, which give trail horses a chance to show off in the ring the skills they have picked up on the trail and be judged for their abilities.

## Arena Habits

Many habits learned in the riding arena don't translate well to the trail. For instance, after years of listening to trainers say, "And let him walk," after Romeo and I had finished a good canter or jumping a course, I got in a bad habit of letting him walk on the buckle right away, as a reward. He, in turn, acquired the bad habit of jerking the reins right out of my hands as soon as he thought it was time for him to stop working and relax. I never addressed this problem, and eventually found that having the reins pulled out of my hands was annoying enough in the ring, but it's actually dangerous on the trail. Some horses are fine walking on the buckle, but Romeo is not one of those horses. I need to be riding him with at least a little bit of contact, even if we're just at the walk. So unlearning that arena habit has been an important part of our enjoying trail riding. (He still does it in the ring, though, and it is still annoying. We're working on it.)

Other arena habits that can be trouble on the trail include using the same pattern for schooling every day. If your horse is accustomed to walk, trot, and canter in both directions every time he comes out of the barn, he may be confused when you head out on the trail and ask him to stay at a working walk most of the time. The more you trail ride, the more he will understand that you have different requests for different times, but varying his routine when you do ride in the ring will probably help as well. Try working on canter transitions, then trotting for a while, before practicing a working walk, and then cantering again.

Walking during schooling is often a break or a reward for some show horses. The rest of us can take a page from the dressage riders' book and work on the quality of our horses' walks. A trail horse should not merely amble down the trail unthinkingly, but should step out in a nice working walk—what Western riders

call a "fence walk," or a walk that would allow you to check fences as you go. A working walk is a gait many horses don't have. Even if trail riding is simply a form of recreation for you and your horse, and you want him to find it relaxing, it is still better for him to pull himself together and walk forward nicely. Concentrating on his work may also help him spook less, since he is thinking about what you are asking of him, just as he would in the ring.

If your horse is a lazy walker, try lungeing him at the walk. Just as you would if he were trotting or cantering, ask him to move forward and watch to see that his hindquarters are engaged and that he is working as he walks. He may try to trot, since a sloppy trot is easier for him to do than an engaged walk, but bring him back down while insisting that he walk on. Once you're on the trail, do plenty of hills, and don't let him trot or lurch up them. Using an energetic walk to climb a hill is excellent exercise for a horse and also keeps him attuned to your requests.

## Start Out in the Ring

If you're lucky enough to be heading out on the trail from a place with a ring, starting in there is a good way to get your horse thinking about the job ahead, and not simply getting excited to be out of the ring. He will understand that trail riding is still a time for him to respond to your aids. Have him concentrate on slowing or stopping with trot-walk and canter-walk transitions, or get his gas pedal unstuck by doing some upward transitions from trot to canter.

Keep working on obedience and response to your requests; for example, trot your horse, then stop a few times until he gets the idea that it is time to listen to your commands. Lots of praise for his obedience will help. Getting your horse in the mindset of paying attention before you really need him to will help both of you once you are out on the trail. Then, when you need him to work through a tight trail, or stop short, he will be attuned to you and ready to work.

## The Importance of Fitness

No matter your discipline or level of competition, fitness for you and your horse is important. Before starting a fitness program to help your horse in his sport with trail riding and conditioning, talk to your veterinarian first. She can gauge his preparedness to undertake the kind of training you have in mind, and help you set some goals for his progress. Be very clear about the tasks that you want your horse to do, such as jumping or lateral movements. Then ask your veterinarian what exercises can strengthen the muscles involved in your sport.

Horses are generally willing to do what is asked of them, which is why your veterinarian's assurance that what you ask your horse to accomplish is reasonable. Keep hill climbing to a minimum if your horse has been out of work for a while. If he tends to be heavy on the forehand, hill work will be all the harder for him, so this is where good dressage training can really come in handy. Your horse should travel using his hind end, especially when he goes down a hill. You will be able to feel his "engine" as you go downward smoothly instead of in a jerky fashion, as a horse on the forehand will do. Also, plan to walk downhill. Trotting down hills is really best saved for horses in good shape who are used to it.

Trotting up them is good for anyone, though, especially when done at a steady and even pace.

Conditioning programs vary widely depending on the sport. A reasonable goal for most horses is to walk a mile in ten minutes, or to step out at about 6 miles per hour. A horse who can move easily at this rate is in decent condition. If you want to participate in a particularly physically demanding sport like three-day eventing or endurance riding, your horse will require a more tailored conditioning program. At this level, you will probably have a trainer who will design a more formal and specific training program for each event you plan to compete in.

Lungeing is often used to settle a trail horse before he goes out, to make him less hyper and more able to focus. It helps any horse get into better condition and conquer the trail or the ring. Too much lungeing can make a horse sour and uneven, but it is a good way to add "miles" at different paces, because it requires aerobic and anaerobic strength to move in a small circle on the lungeline. Twenty minutes is enough time to work a horse and prevent him from getting too bored.

Side reins can help build the rear muscles your horse needs to collect and carry himself. To get your horse more used to trail riding and its uneven footing, don't only lunge him in the ring. Taking him out to a field can help him be more surefooted and used to the idea when you ride him on similar ground. But always use full lungeing equipment, like a lungeing cavesson. And never lunge your horse from his bridle, even in the most casual circumstance. A halter slipped over the bridle, while not ideal, will at least prevent you from pulling on his mouth and hurting him, which can happen with a lungeline clipped to the bit.

To get a show horse used to riding in the ring ready for the trail, plenty of walking and trotting will be the basis of his conditioning. This is when that working or fence walk comes in handy. Start out moving him along for fifteen or twenty minutes, and then each day, add on five more minutes. After concentrating on the walk, start walking for about five minutes, then trotting for a while until you are balancing walking for ten minutes with trotting for ten minutes.

Keep in mind the importance of trail and field riding for conditioning. Trail rides may not just be time off from schooling— they may offer the same benefits for strength and fitness that schooling does, with the added advantage of giving you and your horse a break from routine. Trails and fields can offer excellent muscle-building opportunities with hill work and varying terrain.

Especially for an equine athlete, periods of down time are important. One day a week without being ridden at all is good for horses, and while you are riding on the trail, give him some time off, too. Just because you are concentrating on fitness does not mean that you can't stop and enjoy the view occasionally or have a picnic once in a while. It will give him a chance to catch his breath and both of you the opportunity to gather energy for the rest of the ride.

One special note about seasons: even the most dauntless riders and competitors among us tend to ride less during the winter. Forbidding weather keeps us inside and off our horses more than we would like. So when the sun starts shining again, and the weather gets beautiful, we want to get out and ride all the time. Spring can be one of the best (and easiest) times of year to ride. You don't have to fuss with blanketing, and can often skip the rituals of the post-ride hose down and pre-ride and turnout fly spray.

If you have been riding all winter, your horse is probably still in great shape and ready to go for a long spring ride. Many riders, however, push their horses (and themselves) too much during this season, especially if they did not ride all winter. They're so excited to get back in the saddle, they head out for long rides without heeding their horse's lack of fitness. Gradual reconditioning is the best way to get your horse fit again.

Riders need to take it gradually as well. Do stretching exercises in the days before your first long trail ride, and make sure that you're in shape to do it. Once you are out on the trail, change positions often as you ride. Stand in your stirrups, post the trot, anything to keep you moving and get you out of being cramped into the same position, which can only lead to soreness. Kick your feet out of your stirrups periodically as well. Do ankle turns and point your toes up and then down. Change your stirrup length if necessary as well. You don't need to have your legs hiked up as if you're about to jump. Let them be a little longer than usual. If you get really stiff, hop off and walk your horse for a while. It's good for both of you.

This is no day to try a new pair of jeans or boots. Wear an old outfit you know you're comfortable in. For the first week, stick to the arena or fields, just taking short rides with some walking and trotting. It's a good idea to ride frequently this week, even though each ride may only be about twenty minutes long. You can even do lunge work. By the next week, add some hills, and do longer periods of trotting. Riding five days this second week will keep your horse improving and getting closer to a goal of longer trail rides.

## Your Horse's Weight

Before beginning any kind of conditioning program, your horse's weight should be ideal. And as you work him, it's important to pay attention to his weight. Most pasture horses are heavy in the fall and slimmer after the wintertime, but even with some variation, your horse needs to maintain an appropriate weight, or stay in good flesh. Since we can't easily ask them to hop on a scale, and the weight estimation tapes are notoriously unreliable, eyeballing is still one of the best ways to gauge weight. Even though the main goal of conditioning is to improve strength and stamina, not to regulate weight, a horse will have a much easier time staying fit if he is in good flesh.

One way to monitor weight visually is to look at your horse's back. It should be fairly level, or even have a slight crease. (The old adage is that you can roll an egg down the middle of a fit horse's back.) A little rib—perhaps where the ribcage ends—is all right, but not too much should be showing. An "average" horse will have a level back. In an underweight horse, the back bone is prominent, and perhaps the hip bones or pelvic bones as well.

If your horse is too fat, he can struggle just as much as one who is too skinny. The crease down the horse's back will become deeper, and the area at the top of his tail will seem pudgy. Over-

This horse is on the slender side, but not too thin. His ribs are just showing as he walks, and his gleaming coat suggests good health.

weight horses stress their joints and heart. Founder, or laminitis, is a real danger for the overweight horse. Along with giving him more activity, you should help a horse lose some of his extra weight by putting him in a dry sandlot for some of the day, or cutting down his rations. His joints will support him better as well as get him back into last summer's girth.

## Rider Fitness

Being "riding fit" is an important fitness qualification for trail riding and other horse sports, and for trail riders, cardiac fitness is helpful if they plan to do a lot of riding at speed. Otherwise, trail riding is a fairly laid-back venture as far as getting winded is concerned, but riding muscles—especially those in the legs and back—need to be in shape, or each ride will end in soreness and pain. The days when riders got their only exercise from riding are over. Now, most competitive riders spend time in the gym, weight training and improving their cardiac fitness.

Being overweight is, of course, not ideal. Extra weight increases the strain on your joints, and adds to your horse's burden. Riding, however, is one sport that is not entirely hostile to overweight athletes. A heavy rider can do just fine, as long as she is in decent shape and her horse is well-proportioned.

Many bigger riders like bigger horses for the congruent image they present. They feel that a larger horse complements their own body build. If they are short-coupled and strong, even dainty Arabians and sturdy smaller ponies can carry heavy riders. A horse with serious conformation flaws, however, will probably be better off with a lighter weight rider like a child or a petite adult.

Regardless of your weight, you owe it to your horse to stay in good physical condition. A horse will perform better carrying a fit rider. Someone in shape is less likely to slam down onto his back, and less likely to try to hold herself up with the reins, both of which can bother and hurt a horse. Being in riding shape also makes you a better, more balanced, rider. Talent goes a long way, but even someone born with a great feel for a horse and soft hands gets tired and more likely to slop around in the saddle when she's not in shape. And riding for a long time, as many trail riders do, is tiring. When you are fit, a long ride does not take so much out of you. Riding at speed is particularly fatiguing—especially if you are in a two-point or galloping position—but easier if you are used to it and in good cardiac health.

You may decide that you need to get in better shape after coming home from the barn stiff and sore one too many times. Ask your doctor to suggest exercises that will help alleviate a particular problem. Joint pain—especially in the knee and ankle—is a common complaint. Riders with back pain may benefit from back braces made for people with weak abdominal muscles, as they can stabilize the area. Braces can also help people trying to get back into riding shape, for example, women who have had Caesarean sections. Braces and wraps for legs and ankles (not entirely unlike horses' wraps) can help, but keeping the joints strong with a weight-bearing exercise regimen is even better.

Riding sometimes produces back pain, with causes ranging from tension to poor position. Certain body types can predispose riders to back pain as they ride. Women who are top-heavy may notice more back pain, and a good sports bra can help with this. Women who wear high heels to work may find that switching to lower heels will give their backs a rest. Riders carrying extra weight elsewhere may also suffer from lower back pain, because it is harder for them to ride in a good position.

Centered Riding and Connected Riding are among many teaching styles that focus on avoiding back pain-causing tension, so if you can find a trainer who works within one of these systems, she may help you to find ways to ride without straining yourself. Since tension is such a common cause of back pain, changing your riding style or simply adding a new instructor may help.

It's also easy to strain your back when you are working around the barn. Pay attention as you care for your horses, using your legs instead of your back, as you do barn chores. Avoid lifting overly heavy loads on your own. Stretching before your ride, even as you groom your horse, can assist your suppleness. Flexibility in your legs and back can make you feel better later.

If you're riding with a sore back, you might notice more pain when sitting the trot, unless your horse has a super-easygoing, Western Pleasure-style trot or jog. Although it seems to require more effort, ride a stronger trot and post to help your back. You need to use control and leg strength, but posting saves your back. Even if you ride Western, posting is easier on your back, especially if you jog for longer lengths of time.

Strength training can help everyone, not just those with previously injured backs. Strengthening and toning exercises like Pilates and yoga can help because they strengthen abdominal muscles. These muscles, in turn, can help support your back while riding.

## Trail Riding While Pregnant

Many show riders turn to the trails when they are expecting a baby, since it seems like a much gentler sport than the jumping or barrel racing they were doing. They may not want to quit riding entirely, but decide that trail riding is the perfect compromise. Riding at a slower pace is less jarring and more comfortable for an expectant mother, and trail riding can be the perfect way to maintain a relationship with your horse while taking a break from more strenuous sports.

As with everything about pregnancy, how long to ride is a very personal decision. Some women stop riding as soon as they hear the news. Others ride through their first or second trimester, and even when they are farther along. Just as women gauge whether a certain horse or jump is safe when they are not pregnant, they must decide what they feel comfortable with as their pregnancy progresses.

If you decide to keep riding during your pregnancy, discuss your plans with your doctor or midwife, making sure they understand precisely what you plan to do. Any exercise involving potential for even mild abdominal trauma like skiing or diving is usually a bad idea. Riding is a physically dangerous activity. Riders run a risk of injury from getting kicked, falling off, and other accidents. To add to the danger, you're not as good a rider when you're pregnant because your joints, including those in the pelvic area, loosen. The balance you've relied on your whole riding life is apt to be far less sharp during pregnancy.

## Endurance Riding

If you want to merge your love of competing on horseback with your desire to trail ride, sports such as endurance riding, ride-and-tie, and competitive trail riding are available to you.

Endurance riding is the apex of competitive trail riding. Featuring many Arabian horses and known for its athletic and idiosyncratic riders, endurance riding is a unique sport in an often formal world of equestrian sports.

Arabians are the horse of choice for endurance riders because they have many large blood vessels close to their skin, which means they can cool down easily. With their desert ancestry, this ability makes the Arabian a natural for a sport that involves a lot of heat. Mustangs, with their tough feet and small, hardy build, also make good endurance horses. Thoroughbreds, although they have

This mule on an endurance ride demonstrates that any type of mount can participate in the sport. (The rider in front should be wearing a helmet, like the riders in the rear.)

enough Arabian in them to cool down rapidly after a workout, have been bred to such a point that their feet have trouble on rocky trails, and Quarter Horses are often considered too muscular to be happy getting so hot so often. However, if your horse, no matter the breed, seems like an endurance candidate, he just may be. Plenty of grade horses have succeeded.

Endurance riding has weight divisions. (The weight refers to the weight of the rider and her tack.) The levels begin at Feather-weight, which is under 160 pounds, and go up to Heavyweight, which is 210 pounds or over. Endurance riding—and indeed, most of the trail sports—has periodic vet checks, or "holds," throughout the event. (The rider's time is held while she is at the vet check. Since riders must wait for every horse at a vet check to be examined, lines can build up and it can take an hour or more for your turn.) At the vet-in, or first of these checks, the vet examines the horse and makes sure the horse is fit to start. Riders carry a vet card with them for the duration of the ride, and each card has categories like impulsion, capillary refill, muscle tone, and overall impression. At each check, the vet makes notes on this card. As you would when renting a car, you note what problems were already there—a scrape he got in the field, for example, or an old windpuff—so that the veterinarian does not think it is a result of particularly hard riding.

A veterinarian checks each horse to make sure his heart rate, temperature, and other vital signs are all normal and holding up, which is no easy feat when you are asking your horse to climb all kinds of terrain and riding at speed. Veterinarians also check for any lamenesses and soundness problems that may be cropping up along the way. But in endurance riding, the horse's condition is as important as when he finishes. In fact, the Best Condition trophy awarded at the end of each race is almost as meaningful as the winner's.

On some endurance rides, time penalties are given for the horse's condition being out of the permitted range. This keeps riders from racing their horses through the vet checks, and makes people think twice before pushing their horses too hard in an effort to make time. On the other hand, many endurance riders consider themselves successful if they finish the ride, and don't worry about their time. Hence the endurance riding motto: "To finish is to win."

Endurance riding does not stop for weather, so riders who started out the day in a tank top may need a raincoat by the first vet check. Also, a ride can take place at different altitudes which could tax riders and horses trying to acclimate themselves to various altitudes. Endurance rides start at 25 miles, to be completed in six hours. This level is often called the Limited Distance Division. To those of us who are not endurance riders, 25 miles seems plenty long, but that's a beginner's race in the endurance world. It takes a lot of time—up to a year or two—to get a horse ready to go 25 miles. The next level is 50 miles, to be completed in twelve hours, and the 100-mile rides have a 24-hour time limit. Some of the latter can be local level while others, like the world famous Tevis Cup race, in California, are international competitions with endurance riders and fans flocking to ride and watch the favorites compete.

Endurance riders have crews, not unlike the pit crews of racecar drivers. These crews help at each vet check or stop, to make sure the horse's condition is all right and assist the rider. They monitor the horse's heart rate with a stethoscope, and help get the horse's heart rate down before the vet check. Crews may notice that if it takes more than ten minutes for the rate to go down, the rider is probably asking too much of her horse. Mainly, crews offer the horse water to drink and hose him down, or sponge him off with Vetrolin® or a cooling solution of alcohol and water. They hose down hot horses so that their temperatures fall within the ride rules. They readjust bandages, and feed horses electrolytes and snacks. Crews also carry items like sunblock, clothes, and water for the riders. At the largest rides, these crews include farriers, equine massage therapists, and many assistants. At the smaller rides, crews often consist of the rider's spouse or friends, and many horses have no crew at all.

A bridge obstacle challenges riders to demonstrate their horses' calm and versatility. (Even though his horse is standing still, the rider observing should have both feet in his stirrups.)

## Competitive Trail Riding

In many ways, competitive trail riding is the kinder, gentler cousin to endurance riding. Like endurance riding, competitive trail riding does not involve the ritual and formality of many equestrian sports. Its competitions are not quite as long or arduous as endurance rides tend to be, which means that some competitors use it as a gateway sport.

The goal is to ride over a 20- to 50-mile course that varies in terrain, and to finish within the time limit. Competitive trail riding judges horses and riders on time, distance, and stress. Unlike endurance riding, speed is not a factor, but there are specified minimum and maximum riding times. Veterinary and horsemanship judges observe how riders handle their horses and how they negotiate natural obstacles. Also, you will find many more breeds represented, as opposed to the Arabian-dominated world of endurance riding. Both events, however, depend upon conditioning for maximum ability to work on hills and varying topography.

The organization hosting the ride determines the basic divisions. The North American Trail Ride Conference, which is one of the largest organizations, divides its riders into the Open Division (for horses 5 years of age and over), Heavyweight (190 pounds and over), Lightweight (100 through 189 pounds), and also fields a Junior Division. Its Competitive Pleasure Division is for horses 4 years and older, and has no age or weight restrictions. The Novice is primarily for horses 4 and older and newcomers to the sport, with the same weight divisions as Open, or Senior/Junior. For the rides, divisions progress in length and pacing so the pace for the Open Division is about 4 to 6 miles per hour on a 25- to 35-mile trail for a one-day ride. For the Novice and Competitive Pleasure Divisions, the pace is about 3½ to 5 miles per hour on a 20- to 25-mile trail for a one-day ride.

The judging team for a competitive trail ride consists of at least one veterinarian. As in endurance riding, factors such as pulse, respiration, and dehydration are checked and used to decide winners. Each horse starts the ride with 100 points. Soundness might count for 45%, while condition counts for 40%, and trail ability and trail manners account for 15%. There is also a horsemanship card with categories like grooming, trail equitation, and trail care, safety, and courtesy. Prizes are awarded in several divisions for different accomplishments.

## Ride and Tie

Ride and Tie combines human trail running and endurance riding. The origins of the sport date back to the time when people relied on horses for transportation, and often two people had only one horse between them, and needed to find a way to share the horse and to get to their destination. Now it's a sport with national associations, and its legitimacy began in 1971, when Levi Strauss sponsored a Ride and Tie event.

A team consists of two people and a horse who travel across a 20- to 100-mile cross-country course by alternating riding and running. The starting line of a Ride and Tie is always a bit wild, as up to 100 riders circle and wait for a one-minute warning and then the starting shot. A lot of dust is kicked up as all the horses start out, so runners wear scarves to protect their faces.

The rider goes down the trail as far as she think her afoot

partner can go. The rider stops and dismounts. She then ties the horse up to a tree, fence post, or perhaps hands the reins to a member of the team's crew in special situations, and starts running. Often, teams decorate their horses with brightly colored leg wraps or grease pencil markings so they are easily found. Teams can switch as much as they like, but usually ride organizers mandate at least six exchanges.

The first (running) team member reaches the horse and rides to catch her partner up ahead. When she reaches the riding member, they can either stop and exchange when they meet (which is called a flying tie), or the rider can take a little more time. Then she ties the horse up and starts running again. There is no proscribed system for when the team members exchange. Instead, the strategy is part of the sport, as each team has to figure out the best way for them to make their way speedily down the trail.

There is a vet check at the halfway point of a Ride and Tie, with many of the same categories evaluated as in an endurance race. The riders exchange at this point, as well. By the end of a Ride and Tie, teams begin to fight each other for finishing places. Usually, teams are competing primarily against their own times and most of all, trying to finish. Although all three members of a team do not have to finish together, they are not counted as having finished until all three have passed the finish line.

The fastest teams in Ride and Tie can average better than 10 miles per hour. Many take approximately 5 to 6 hours to complete a 25-mile race, which is close to a normal walking pace. Ride and Tie is an excellent sport for endurance or competitive trail riders who want to stay in top shape themselves. Riders can also empathize with a horse that is put through serious physical training.

Ride and Tie is also a good way to share a horse. Spouses, children and parents, and friends all make up teams. It's convenient if your teammate is around your height because it means less messing around with stirrups, but it's obviously not the most important thing.

Riders experienced using a compass can combine their skills with horsemanship in competitive mounted orienteering.

## Competitive Mounted Orienteering

The sport of competitive mounted orienteering can be done solo or as part of a team, and involves riding skills as well as compass-reading skills. Each rider receives a map with numbered stations on it, with compass bearings. Riders find each station with their compasses, note the identifying symbol or letters that ride organizers have placed on the station, and return to the start, trying to work as fast as possible. Courses vary in length, with beginners usually riding shorter courses and the longer ones designed for those who have been doing competitive mounted orienteering for some time.

Riders have to plan carefully the best way to ride the course. They can pick up speed between each station, riding slowly when they think they might see a landmark. The landmarks provide the readings that allow the orienteers to find their target stations, which are often simply paper plates. Competitive mounted orienteering aficionados call it "the thinking horse sport." The sport is unrestricted as to breed of horse or type of tack and equipment used.

## Trail Trials

If you're looking for competition different from the show-ring atmosphere of a trail class, but something not as focused on conditioning as the endurance sports, you may be interested in trail trials, which some riders call TT. Taking their name from field trials (also called point-to-points), in which hunters compete on an

Even a log in his path can allow a horse to show his gameness on the trail.

open course over the types of jumps they can expect while hunting, trail trials give trail horses a way to show off in their normal habitat.

Trail trials also offer more leeway than trail classes. Two horses can each score well even if they handle a situation differently. Also, obstacles will be more like those you would see on the trail (obviously, since you are on the trail). Even rotting trash can be an obstacle. Some of the obstacles will even be similar to those in mounted games, such as carrying water or passing hats. A judge stands at each obstacle to rate how the horse and rider do.

Trail trials provide a good way for riders to improve their skills without the show-ring nerves and expense of a trail class.

## Trail Classes

Those who want to showcase their horse's trail abilities and skill without actually hitting the trail can participate in trail classes. Many breed and agricultural youth shows and other horse shows now offer trail classes. These allow trail riders to compete against each other by demonstrating their ability to open gates and mailboxes, and perform other tasks while on horseback. Obstacles including bridges and logs are set out to challenge the horses' trail abilities. Some classes have set time limits and patterns to memorize. As in show jumping, courses vary widely. Trail classes are more commonly seen in Western shows, but are now becoming more frequent in English shows.

Trail classes also have another purpose: it's safer to ride a trail horse who is entirely sure of what he's doing. All the time spent navigating poles and pylons in an arena can only pay off on the trail. A trail horse who's very experienced on real trails will probably not have too much trouble in a trail class, unless he is very unused to crowds and show scenes. The reverse is also true: if a horse can perform all the difficult tasks required to succeed in a trail class, he is probably a wonderful trail horse if he is accustomed to the sights and sounds of the outdoors as well as those of a horse show.

Some sample tasks include opening, passing through, and

closing a gate, carrying objects from one part of the arena to another, riding through water, over logs or "brush," riding down into and up out of a ditch without lungeing or jumping, crossing a bridge, backing through obstacles, sidepassing, mounting and dismounting from either side, passing a slain animal's hide. Other classes might require you to put on or remove a coat, carry an object, make a water crossing, open and close a mailbox, turn, mount and dismount, tie a manger or bowline knot, or ground-tie your horse. Dragging objects or standing quietly while the rider gets off and leads the horse are other tasks. Course designers strive to set the obstacles so that neither a very small nor a very large horse finds them easier. A trail class may also include urban hazards like flags, orange pylons, and city barricades. Even dry ice or fire extinguishers may make an appearance if you are exhibiting at a show with a particularly imaginative course designer.

When mounting or dismounting in a trail class, judges may expect riders to fulfill basic safety and horsemanship tasks like inspecting a girth. Trotting is usually expected to be a sitting trot in a trail class, even for English riders. Crops and whips are not appropriate gear for trail classes. Judges will often take off points for faults such as tail wringing (thought to demonstrate an unhappy or unwilling horse), bit chewing, rushing through the

Mounting and dismounting tests in trail trials show judges how well horse and rider communicate.

course or moving listlessly, falling or stepping off the bridge, refusing an obstacle, stepping outside the markers placed to designate the course, or simply breaking pattern.

Trail class judges also look for surefootedness, since it is such an important quality in a trail horse. A trail pattern may have several logs or rails laid in such a way that the horse must carefully navigate what is on the ground in front of him. Objects like pylons or barrels are also used in trail classes to force the horses to pay attention to the placement of their feet. The "box" is a square intended to demonstrate the horse's nimbleness. He is expected to enter the box and do a full circle without touching the sides. This is where trail classes start veering away from the real thing. Backing is often done along poles placed at 90-degree angles from each other, while keeping your horse from hitting the poles.

Usually, while the horse is going through the pattern, riders are supposed to keep their hands up and off the horse's neck so that the horse, and not the rider, is making decisions. This shows how well his training has paid off. If a horse takes too long negotiating one obstacle, judges will usually ask the rider to move him along to the next one. Breaking the pattern or surmounting obsta-

A "box" tests surefootedness and rider control.

cles out of their posted order can be cause for penalties. For English riders, you may have to practice riding one-handed, a skill Western riders already have. When you need to drag something or open a gate, you will need that hand.

If you are just starting out with a young horse, you may even want to consider in-hand trail classes that are specifically designed for horses not yet trained to be ridden. These classes offer good goals for you to achieve and a way for your baby to learn ground manners. The patterns are usually simple, with tasks like backing up a short way or leading over a bridge. In-hand trail classes give a young horse the means to get some seasoning even before you can get on his back.

To practice at home, you may have to make your own obstacles. Be creative. Haul in big branches with leaves still on them, and lay weighted tarps on the ground. Use poles and a heavy-duty plastic jump block system, and some pylons. You can even make your own bridge out of wooden pallets. If you paint them, put some wet sand or ground gravel in the paint so the horse is less likely to slip. If you know someone with deer decoys or life-size livestock models, you can really simulate what you'll find in the ring.

## Getting Ready

No matter your sport, the guiding principle when getting your horse ready for a competition is to keep things the same as always. Many horses can sense change, and will know they are going to a competition even before you get the trailer hooked up. Horses are sensitive animals, and they can tell when you are gearing up for an unusual activity.

Feeding times and amounts should remain consistent, since this is a physical health matter as well as a mental health one. A horse whose routine gets upset can colic from the stress. Other things to keep the same are tack, shoeing, and his daily routine. A bath is a good idea before a competition. Even though turnout is not part of many trail sports, a clean horse does better under saddle for prolonged periods.

If it is your horse's first time away from home, or if he just tends to be on the finicky side, take food and water with you. The hassle will be worth the peace of mind of knowing, especially, that he will drink and stay hydrated without a fuss.

## Volunteering

If you or your horse are not quite ready to begin competing in one of the trail sports, you can still gain exposure and experience from volunteering at the event. Show managers often can use an extra hand on the day of the ride to hold horses for vet checks or just count heads. Unmounted volunteers can help with food, timing at the beginning and finish of the event, and recording for judges. Volunteers can also work as spotters. They are posted along the trail to count horses and riders. In addition, spotters help riders avoid getting lost, and keep spectators and riders alike on track. Taking horses' pulses and counting respiration is often a volunteer task as well. After the race, volunteers help clean up the trail, so that markers, signs, and food wrappers don't litter the trail for the next riders.

# 4

# **Trail Riding** in Parks and on Paths

City, national, and state parks, where trails are cut and maintained for horses, offer a number of advantages to the rider: picturesque and user-friendly trails, signage, trail maps, and rangers who provide law enforcement and assistance to riders and other park users. Many trails, however, are also shared with hikers and cyclists, which is becoming more common as fewer and fewer bridle paths remain solely for equestrian use. As outdoor sports proliferate, land gets scarcer, and mountain bikers vie for space with horseback riders and Sunday hikers. Riding in parks and on designated bridle paths insures that horses have a place to go, but it no longer means that the paths will be reserved exclusively for horses.

## Trailering to a Park and Parking Lots

Since so few barns border national or state parks, you may be hauling your horses or having them hauled so you can ride there.

Park your trailer where regulations specify.

Parks with bridle paths usually have designated parking areas for trailers. Be sure to heed posted rules and notices about trailers. Don't leave any horses unattended in the trailer while you are riding or elsewhere in the park. Someone should stay with them so that if anything happens help is readily available. Also, don't gather in a parking lot with your riding companions while you're waiting for everyone in your group to get ready. Move off to the side so that when new trucks and trailers come in, they have plenty of room to park and unload.

## Basic Trail Sharing

There are differing schools of thought about encountering back-packers or bicyclists on the riding trail. Some horse people feel that trails should not have to be shared at all, and prefer to ride only on trails designated solely as bridle paths. It helps to be open-minded about sharing since you'll have a wider variety of places to ride if you accustom your horse to what is out there. (See Chapter 2 for advice.) Your horse may spook when, for example, he sees a recumbent bicycle or something else for the first time, but as with other scary items, he will be less alarmed by

A kind word or a chat with hikers using the same trail as you are will make them more inclined to be accepting of riders.

the second and third encounter. Once he relaxes, you will be more inclined to be relaxed yourself.

Show politeness toward people you meet on the trail whether or not they are riding. Smile and wave at passersby. (Saying hello has a safety aspect as well, because if a hiker speaks to you, it will reassure your horse that he is just another person instead of a giant-backed monster.) Also, watch out for people who are unused to horses and think they are helping you out by hiding behind a tree. They may believe that this will make the horse walk on by, when you know that such behavior will make your horse more skittish when he has to start worrying whether the person will jump out. Say hello, and see if you can get the hiker to announce himself and reassure your horse that he is, in fact, just another person. You might even have to gently point out to the hiker that concealing himself is more likely to upset your horse than standing out in the trail.

## Hitching Posts

One of the nice things about trail riding in a park as opposed to riding on privately held land is that there are likely to be rider conveniences, like the hitching post or rail that is at least chest high for comfort. A horse should be tied at withers height, or higher. If he's tied this high he will probably not hurt his neck if he pulls back. A drawback to hitching rails is that your horse can slide his lead rope along it to get some grass or get next to another horse.

Watch the length of your lead rope, too. It needs to be long enough to keep the horse's head in a natural position. He'll get sore if his head is hiked up, and if he can get the rope all the way down to the ground, he could step over it and hurt himself.

Some parks will have overhead cables to which you can tie your horse. These are strong cables suspended between two strong trees. While horse campers have to figure out how to attach their horse without the knot sliding down the cable, parks with overhead cables will have permanent tie ropes so that you can fasten your horse's halter without too much trouble.

Many parks require riders to use tree saver straps. Check the signage. You could be in for a fine if a ranger finds your horse is not tied to a tree with a tree saver strap. Most trail riding outfitters sell these straps, and it's a good idea to use them on all trees, not just those in parks.

## Historic Trails

Trail riding often allows you to experience historical sites firsthand. When you're on horseback, you see the land as the people who made it historical did. Whether the park is a battleground or the site of a famous gathering, you and your horse are following in the steps of previous generations. More than driving and sometimes even more than hiking, riding can evoke a personal connection to the past.

When you ride in a historic area, treat it as you would a wilderness area you were aiming to leave untouched. Take pictures, but nothing else from the site. (If you think you may be the first to see it, consider telling a local historical or archaeological society.) Don't remove any artifacts. Signs will often be posted, but it is a good practice to keep as far from active research

These signs indicate clearly that no horses are permitted on this trail.

sites as possible. If you see that metal detecting is forbidden in a certain area, then there are artifacts present and they are supposed to stay where they are.

Be careful around historic sites, especially if you are not on a well-traveled park path. Hazards like wells or barbed wire can be buried under years of detritus and leaves. Old building sites may look sturdy, but not be up to bearing the weight of your horse. If you know something about botany, the flora that surrounds an area may tell you if people used to live there. Non-native plants, especially if they are decorative, can signify that someone once lived and gardened on the site you're riding on.

**Everyday Trail Riding**

Ranger programs are particularly valuable in historic parks, where one spot may closely resemble another unless you are with a person who knows which battle was fought where, or where a certain homestead or gravesite used to be. Riding along with a ranger can also alleviate fears you may have about disturbing historical sites. It's also worthwhile to read up on a historic site before you ride it, since it will give you a understanding of what you're seeing.

## Finding Your Way

Often trees are marked or "blazed" with paint to designate which path is which. In some cases, all the equestrian trails will be marked with one shape while hiking trails will have another symbol, which makes it easier to ensure that you are not wandering off the horse trail. Although some trails are marked, you could possibly confuse a designated trail with a wildlife trail. Carry a park topographic map, often found at a ranger station, and compass. Leave your trip itinerary with someone at the station so she can contact help if you are overdue.

This trail map is at a convenient height for riders. (McGraw photo)

Reading trail maps requires close attention because different colors may be used to mark each kind of trail. Equestrian trails may be blue, while hiking trails are red, and so on. Or equestrian trails may be represented by a dotted line while hiking trails are solid. Familiarize yourself with the riding trails before you set out so that you know where you're going as you ride. Keep a copy of the trail map with you in a pocket or pommel bag, and refer to it often.

Maps may be posted at various places along the trails and in parking or picnic areas, which makes things even more convenient. Be responsible for knowing where you are. It's tough to blame others for your horse bolting if you did not look to see that you were heading onto a golf course.

## Backcountry Riding

The term "backcountry" has a different meaning for different parks, but in general, the backcountry is an area unpatrolled and unserviced by rangers or other park employees. Backcountry camping usually means camping without a campground, and backcountry hiking typically means there are no trails.

Following posted arrows lets you know that you are obeying a landowner's wishes when you ride his property.

**Everyday Trail Riding**

Following rules in whichever park you are riding in is very important. Often, horses are not allowed on the roads that traverse parks or in campgrounds and picnic areas, while larger parks may have horse campgrounds in which you are welcome to ride.

If you do plan backcountry camping and riding, you may need a permit which specifies, among other things, length-of-stay limitations, limits on the number of horses allowed, and whether hobbles are required. And be sure to check that your hay and feed is free of weeds so that exotic plants don't threaten local ones.

## Manure

It's obviously impractical for trail horses to wear the "tail bags" many urban carriage horses wear. But as horsekeepers, we know what a problem manure can be. Horses produce tons of it, and we spend hours hauling it away, finding mushroom farms to come get it, harrowing, and composting it. On the other hand, because manure is a fact of sharing life with horses, we deal with it.

Manure, however, is one of the first things non-horsepeople notice and complain about when having to share their trails with horses. Many people who share trails wish riders would remove manure, particularly around picnic areas and campgrounds, but it's not always possible. In some places, you are required to remove manure in areas horses congregate. This may mean it goes into a bucket in your horse trailer, or that people who use the same areas pool resources to have the manure hauled away. If manure can be composted on site at the park, it makes things easier for all involved.

If your horse pauses and lifts his tail while you are crossing a stream, try to get him to move along and choose another spot on the trail. Urine and fecal matter harm the fish and other creatures who live in the water, as well as anyone who may drink the water further down the line. Fortunately, horses usually give plenty of warning when they are about to urinate, and most do not prefer more splashing than is necessary, so they probably won't choose a stream. If yours does, gently ask him to move along and find him another quiet place so that he does not contaminate the water source.

## Trail Building

Trails are better both for the environment and to ride if they are built with these goals in mind. Horses accelerate soil erosion, for example, so horse trails should be built so that slope and water conditions are taken into consideration. A path that goes straight downhill will not easily stay intact, because the steeper the area, the more a trail will erode as rainwater washes over it. Next thing you know, there is a moatlike channel running down the middle of the hill, which everyone steps to the side to avoid. Now you have much more impact than is necessary. Trails do better if they zigzag a bit. (It's easier on the horses, too.)

Any trail built on a flood plain, or over a spring, will always be mucky and wet. It will suck horseshoes off, and also encourage riders to go around it and hack even more of a path. It's true that paths may go through flood plains because when they follow a stream, riders are less likely to get lost. But now that we know how building over wet areas harms the trails, it's best to find another way.

In general, the more riders get involved at the planning stage, the better the trails and the riding will be. If you regularly ride in the same areas, get involved. Go to planning council and zoning committee meetings to represent equestrian issues, which will be good for you and other riders who enjoy the same land.

## Seasonal Issues

Parks may have different rules and regulations depending upon the season. In an effort to preserve the wilderness around trails, some parks do not open their trails until the local rainy season has passed. This keeps horses away when there is the most mud and the greatest likelihood that horses will slide around or that riders will create new damage in an effort to avoid the mud.

## Rangers

Park rangers are excellent resources for riders. They ride the park every day in every weather and season, so they know all about the terrain, which spots have the best views, and which are the most enjoyable or safest trails to ride. They can tell you where to cross the water you may encounter, and whether or not it is snake season. They may lead seminars on their parks, and some may even lead trail rides.

Rangers are there primarily to keep the parks safe, so don't be surprised if you are reprimanded for breaking safety rules, such as no glass in a campground, no gaits faster than a trot, or no riding on nature trails. Although some of the rules may seem excessive, it's best to stay on the side of the rangers and obey the limits set by the park.

It is easy to get defensive when people discuss how much horses impact trails. As your horse walks gently along on a pretty day, it's tough to feel as if you are destroying anything. But trails

Obey the seasonal or weather-related rules that are posted to protect trails.

do tend to get ruined by horses over time, depending on their material, hilliness, soil, drainage, and vegetation. Horses tend to compact trails by mashing down vegetation as they walk, and by kicking up top layers of soil. Park staff may try to help the trails stay solid by grading them or rolling them. But trails do get deeper and deeper the more horses are on them, which basically means that the earth is more and more gouged. (See Chapter 6 for more on environmentally friendly trail riding.)

## Easements

An easement is an area that may be on private property, but is still used as a trail. Landowners donate or dedicate easements, and other times they convey from owner to owner with the property. Local authorities, like departments of parks, decide what responsibilities and liabilities this entails. (As with everything equestrian, insurance is a big issue when it comes to easements.) Usually, the county or state is not responsible for anything that happens on the trail because of an owner's carelessness. (For example, if a horse got hurt because of a rusted harrow left on the easement trail.) Attractive nuisances (like a swimming pool) and animal attacks are also usually not something riders can sue the landowner over.

In some areas, conservation easements—which come about when a landowner agrees to preserve her own lands—are popular. Conservation easements do keep property taxes down because they slow development. So for the landowner who is not interested in developing her land, but wants to see it remain unspoiled, a conservation easement can keep her taxes down and allow her to protect the land at the same time.

Easements are a reason to be sure you know where you are riding. If you are not on a trail designated for riding, and something happens, as a trespasser you will have no rights under the law. Stick to familiar spots and places you know have been set aside for riders.

People who own land that they intend to allow equestrians to use do have to care for the land. But the liability protection typically vanishes if the owner charges money to use the trail. The best way to avoid any problems is to have good lines of communication between the landowner and the trail riding group.

Litter on horse trails is unacceptable. If you have even so much as a wrapper from an energy bar, put it back in your saddle pad pocket or jeans pocket and throw it away when you get to a trash can. Nothing shuts down a bridle path faster than trash.

## Signage

Obeying signs posted in parks or on bridle paths is very important. The universal symbol of a circle with a slash through it (like a Do Not Enter sign) is often used to tell riders where they can or cannot ride. As appealing as the hiking or cycling trails may look, stay off them when you see the sign forbidding horses. Assume that a very good reason exists for prohibiting them, such as environmental protection or simply the fact that too many users would crowd the trail. You can't get too irritated at that hiker with the off-leash dog if you are encroaching on her space in the first place. Remember that if you are riding on a bicycle path and a cyclist swerves too close or acts rude, you cannot complain.

Some trails are horse trails only at certain times of the day, and are closed to equestrian traffic other times. And many trails (and parks) are closed before dawn and after dusk. Remember, some parks levy fines against people who disobey the signage. So read carefully and heed what you see on those signs.

## Trail Crime

Trails in parks may have the same crime problems that unfortunately plague the rest of society. While you may feel invulnerable when you are mounted, there is always the daunting possibility that someone will attack you when you are out riding. (Another good reason not to ride alone, especially in an area in which you feel unsafe.)

As rare as muggings of mounted riders are, you should keep in mind these tips if someone on the ground threatens or confronts you. Urging your horse to gallop off is a good idea and will put distance between you and the aggressor. Even a speedy trot can disarm someone unused to horses who may have been considering approaching you. Don't let just anyone pat your horse, because it could lead to you or his bridle being grabbed. You can always tell the person that your horse isn't friendly, and then speed off. Try to keep your horse between you and anyone you find sketchy, and most of all, act confident. You are the one on horseback, and if you follow your instincts, you should be able to escape an unmounted aggressor.

## Activism

Even if local politics do not interest you, as a trail rider you may find yourself embroiled in more controversy than you had bargained for the first day you saddled up and headed out. Unlike those who only ride in arenas, trail riders need scarce open spaces and trails. If your favorite trail is threatened with closing, or a change of use (such as a bridle path turning into a no-horses-allowed bike path), it will be up to you and your fellow riders to speak up for those who use the trail.

Forming a trail group is one way to be heard. Particularly if it involves representatives from other trail user groups—hikers, bikers, cross-country skiers—your group can make an impact, giving the planning board or committee in your area suggestions, just as departments of transportation do. Land trusts and conservation groups can all use an equestrian point of view—and demonstrations of caring about the trail—to understand the importance of building and maintaining trails. Conservation groups may want to hear that you understand the problems facing the trails in question—most likely erosion, to which horses contribute. Although you can always find a study that says that bikers do more damage than horses, or hikers do more damage than horses, it's best to band together with these other groups and find ways to mitigate erosion through proper planning and maintenance.

Go to meetings. It is hard to complain too much when you

try to go for a ride one day and find your favorite trail barricaded if you haven't made any effort to find out what is happening to trails in your area. Read local horse publications, and keep abreast of the controversies that arise over various trails and who may use them.

Make sure you know how horses are being described. If they are, for example, classified as "high impact" on certain trails, this could mean these trails are closed to horses. An argument can be made for horses as low impact, since they don't tear up the paths as much as motorized vehicles do. They can, however, be more destructive than hikers or cross-country skiers, for example, and consequently earn a bad reputation.

If you are lobbying a private citizen to allow horse trails on her property, know exactly what is involved. Many landowners are, understandably, worried about the legal ramifications of people horseback riding on their property. Will they be held responsible if a rider gets hurt on their land? The answer to this question depends upon the situation and the area, so being prepared to respond to a concern will help you when talking to landowners. Recreational use laws exist to help landowners, because unless the landowner charges a fee, she is typically not held liable for an accident on her property. Proper signage and knowledge can assuage fears and let people know that just because someone is riding on their property does not make them legally responsible.°

## Fundraising Trail Rides

If you have a favorite trail that you and your friends want to help maintain, or to help generate publicity to save it or keep it a horse trail, hosting a trail ride can be a great way to get attention and funds. Hosting an event means extra work for everyone, but the payoffs can be tremendous when a formerly moribund trail is back in the news, or a trail that was slated to be for bikes only reverts to multi-use. Local press often covers these types of events, and can garner publicity for your cause. And these events are fun; you get to meet all kinds of like-minded riders, and raise money and awareness for your trail system.

Non-riders can be some of your best allies in the fight to keep trails open.

Hosting a trail ride is a big responsibility. You have to get permits and permissions from local authorities and landowners. Ride the trails yourself, and get them ready for a big group by grooming them, trimming branches, and laying down extra gravel if you need to. Figure out how many people and horses you can host—how many trailers will fit in the parking lot? How many horses can comfortably ride the trail at one time? Keep riding the trail so that you can anticipate any problems. If it has been raining a lot, and some patches of the trail are turning into puddles, you may need to spread some gravel.

Enlist someone in your group who is familiar with administrative tasks to do the registration. The fees will go toward the supplies you need for the ride with the remainder earmarked for the cause. Make sure everyone has directions and information about the trail ride, and make maps for the trail itself. As you ride the trail closer to the day of the ride, you can make signs and markers for the trail as you go. You want to do everything in your power to keep people from getting lost—especially when many of them do not know the trail. One wayward rider can easily lead to dozens on a big trail ride. When the ride begins, you and the other members of your group should help any local authorities to keep things running smoothly by guiding trailers and riders, and helping clean up the trash that piles up along the way.

If you are trying to save a trail that is currently closed to riders, you may (obviously) not be able to host a trail ride on it. If your plan was to alert riders and non-riders to the trail closing, though, there are other ways to heighten awareness and raise money if a lack of funds was responsible for the closing. Stick with a horse theme, and depending on your budget, you can manage anything from a county fair type of event with pony rides and a bake sale to a concert or ball. Since trail riding is out of the question, have a horseless trail ride, with riders dressing in riding clothes and hiking along the trail one day to demonstrate that something is missing. Whatever you believe your community will respond to is best, because your goal is to gain support for your cause and let whichever authorities closed the trail know that there are involved and invested equestrians who want their trails back.

Times like these are when it pays off to have been polite about sharing a trail. If you and other riders are barred from a trail that will remain open to bikers or hikers, enlist the leadership of their groups to help you, as they would no doubt hope for the same if their constituencies were forbidden to use the trail. Who knows which hiker will remember that you took the time to say hello and let a child pat your horse? She could be the leader of a hiking group that may have the ear of the trail use committee.

## Multi-Use Concerns

As a horseperson, you may find it hard to imagine what people are scared of when they are asked to share their hiking, biking, or other park activity with horses and riders. But there are plenty of legitimate concerns that non-equestrians have, some legal and some social. Many have to do with events being held at a park, where horsepeople would veto certain things—like a hot air balloon race, for example—because it could scare horses. Other events, like marathons or large picnics, may also pose concerns for non-equestrians. Even though these sorts of events don't take place on the bridle paths per se (except the marathons), their participants would not want to take horses into consideration when planning.

To allay these reasonable concerns, tout the ability of riders to know their own horses, and concentrate on publicity for any event. You would not want the park thronged with a fundraising tricycle race on the same day as a trail trial, so groups can work together to assure one another that once in a while, their constituents can stay away. If there is a cross-country run one day, the trail could be closed to horse traffic, and if there is an equine event another day, cyclists could be asked to refrain from using the trails.

Park management, even people who ride themselves and have no problems with horses using the trails, can also feel uneasy about horses if there is a large gathering, such as an organized trail ride, in the offing. One concern is that others at the park that day would constitute spectators, and in insurance terms, the park authorities could be liable for injuries incurred by a runaway horse or other equine-related hazards.

Promises of basic risk management should comfort all parties involved. The organized trail ride should probably not muster right by a soccer field or other park facility, and the amateur rocket launchers should be asked to find a site well away from the horse trail. All groups should have to register dates and times with the park authorities, who can then head off any clashing events. Once it's understood by everyone that all groups are subject to the same rules, they should be able to share a park space.

## Volunteer Work

Almost all park authorities benefit from volunteer programs. To heighten your visibility and help secure support from your local park authority, you can volunteer to perform tasks from giving talks on trail sharing to groups of hikers or bikers to picking up trash (nobody's favorite, but always sure to make a big difference).

Some areas have a volunteer ranger program. Through intensive training and time with the real rangers, volunteer rangers help to keep the riding trails safe. Volunteer rangers in the state of Maryland, for example, attend a formal training session. Volunteers learn about environmental protection, resolving conflicts within and among groups, protection of national resources, and even role-playing to learn to deal with situations that arise on their watch. They also learn first aid and CPR. Some of the Maryland rangers' jobs include using two-way radios, dealing with animals and traffic, and protecting natural resources. Their volunteer mounted patrol goes through a more intensive training and works from their own horses as extra eyes and ears for park law enforcement.

In other regions, volunteers for parks might teach classes to non-equestrians about dealing with horses, mediate conflicts between various trail use groups, and help with events at the park, including traffic control. Any opportunity to give back to a park system that has given riding time and space is a good one, so trail riders often help make up these volunteer groups.

## Unused Trails

You might find yourself in the saddle one day, staring at a trail map and wondering why on the map a certain trail looks viable, but as you stare down it, all you see are brambles and vines. So you move on.

Although it is easy to skip an untended trail, don't forget about it. As trails go without traffic, they are more likely to be forgotten about until someone takes the time to groom them and make them more rideable. In many cases, the park authorities will send a crew to do just that once they have a report of the neglected trail, but you may need to volunteer time or support in order to have it done. Park authorities get so busy that if people do not draw their attention to a trail that has gotten overgrown, it might just continue to get more and more buried until it is virtually unusable. Consider it your responsibility to let the rangers or other administrators know just where the trail is and what is happening with it, and you may find yourself with a whole new place to ride.

## Developers

The amount of housing eating up land that was once peaceful and bucolic demonstrates that it is hard to forecast the future. Conservationists thought they were doing an amazing job of preservation when they had counties zone their lots at three acres. At the time, when houses were much smaller, three acres seemed like enough to preserve a quiet country feeling. But then the houses got so much bigger that three acres only allowed for a small lawn around a huge house, along with its garages and swimming pool. It's impossible to see what trends lie ahead. As sad as it can be for those of us who enjoy rural riding, sometimes the pressures of maintaining a farm can be too much for the farmer to bear, and he has to sell his property. When it goes to a developer, who is so frequently the highest bidder, views, trails, and scenery are going to change.

Trail riders and developers are sometimes at odds. When a

formerly rural parcel that had trails and quiet country lanes on it gets sold to a developer, riders naturally tend to fear that they will never be able to use those trails again. And while it is true that you may have to give up your formerly isolated road for an area with families and cars, if you foster a good relationship with the developer, you may find that you have more access than you imagined. Some developments are even billed as equestrian communities, with boarding facilities and trails that delineate the property. But your riding life will certainly be upended, both during the construction of the development and once it is completed and the houses sold. If you're committed to staying and riding on the land, you will have to do some legwork to make sure that you still can.

The earlier you can get involved, the better. This way, you will not only know what is going on, you may even have a say in the plans. In America, a typical desirable ratio is 10 acres of parkland per 1,000 people, and this parkland is both open space and parks. A problem trail riders face is that planners think "horses,"

Building developments and horses can coexist peacefully if there's understanding on both sides. (McGraw photo) and can only envision the acres and acres of rolling pastureland that trail riders will demand. This makes them shut out the idea of trails. While wide open spaces may have been the first choice of equestrians, when faced with serious development, they would rather keep their trails and be able to ride than have nothing. Open fields may be clear examples of local green space, but planners may overlook smaller wooded areas that could be perfectly good horse trails even without hundreds of preserved acres, so it becomes the job of trail riders to alert them to the presence of trail-appropriate land.

During development planning is another time that having been a valued part of a multi-use trail community will serve you well. When you are hawking your idea about placing a new bridle path along the perimeter of a new subdivision, a hiking or preservation group may join forces with you and help you out if they can be sure of your support in sharing that trail and helping with others.

Being a regular attendee at neighborhood meetings can be the only way you find out about what is happening to your trails. In order to ensure an easement through a new development, for example, you would probably need to know well in advance of a project actually starting. Allies can be land conservation groups and zoning boards, with whom contractors and developers have to contend before they start work. Once construction has begun, though, the chances that you will be able to have the property owners consider an equestrian easement decrease. Keep abreast of neighborhood happenings as much as you can, preferably before that first surveyor's stake goes up. It's amazing how much seems to be a "done deal" even before the first load of dirt is hauled away.

During construction, you will have to navigate the existence of scary machines making loud noises all day and constantly changing the way things look to your horses. Construction noises are harsh and unpleasant to people, but they can be terrifying to horses. You might have to wait to ride the property in question until the houses have gone up so that your horses don't become so frightened by bulldozers, backhoes, and dump trucks that they bolt in an increasingly dangerous area littered with machinery and trash. Also, construction sites tend to be muddy, which means your footing is probably unsafe. Now is the time to make yourself known to the contractors. If you keep an open mind and a pleasant demeanor, they may help you by giving you timetables so that you know when you can expect work to be finished.

If you ride at a barn adjoining a rising development, your new neighbors may become a problem when they realize that living next door to a horse farm is not all watching horses graze and gambol peacefully in the mist. They have to smell manure and, if their property includes an easement, allow horses (and their manure) in their backyards or on a path adjoining those backyards. Ideally, with mutual understanding, any differences can be worked out. Your barn may have to contact a mushroom farmer to have more manure hauled off, and the neighbors may have to learn to enjoy the rural feel of people riding nearby, but harmony can be achieved. If your neighbors really protest the quotidian workings of a horse farm that was there before they were, however, you may need to look into your area's Right to

If your horse is in the suburbs, don't close your mind to riding near quiet roads. They're not the woods, but can still offer pleasant rides.

Farm laws. These laws protect farmers and other agricultural groups (including horse owners) from having to alter everything for the new development. Right to Farm laws, which sometimes include agreements that people sign before moving into a development near a horse farm, can help them understand that flies and manure are part of the bargain that includes the beautiful sight of being near horses.

Another problem for trail riders near a new development is the impact it has on the other animals in the area. From deer to squirrels, animals respond to something as major as a development going up. As they are run off their homes and their dens are ravaged, raccoons and possums may head for your barn, so keep sweet feed locked up tight and make sure all the horses are current on their rabies shots.

## Usage

When you are exploring a new neighborhood to see where there are likely places to ride, you need to check into a few things. For one, what is the zoning? Zoning covers what the land can have on it in the future, not just what is there now. Land that is zoned for commercial use can have a house on it, so asking the current property owners about riding on their land may not do very much good in a few years when it becomes a grocery store parking lot.

Ordinances can be another headache. An ordinance is a local law or restriction, which may say, for example, that no livestock (which generally includes horses, even horses being ridden) can enter a certain subdivision. Even if landowners are theoretically amenable to having you ride on their land, if an ordinance forbids it, you may do better to concentrate on riding elsewhere.

# Trail Manners
# and **Riding** in a Group

5

U nlike foxhunting, polo, stadium jumping, and other formal equestrian sports, trail riding does not have a firm code of etiquette. Yet systems are in place that make trail riding more pleasant and safe for everyone, and trail riders heed them. Communication is the key to manners in the world of trail riding. Whether you are asking your partner if she's ready to turn back or deciding whether to canter up a hill with five or six buddies behind you, communicating your intentions—and asking if they suit others—will mean you are acting mannerly as well as safely.

## Barn Manners

Whenever you are a guest at another barn, whether it is public or private, you and your horse should be on your very best behavior. Before you take up any space, ask where you should put your trailer and your horse. When you leave, clean up any mess you made, and thank your hosts for letting you and your horse use their facilities.

Keep to these manners at your own barn. Many trail riders begin their day—or at least their ride—at a boarding barn. If you have your own farm, you don't have to deal with other people and their preferences around your horses. But many of us board our horses, and sometimes we get so comfortable with our own boarding barns that we forget to mind our manners. We like to feel casual as we talk to friends and relax with our horses. And for many of us, our barns are like our second homes. But barns need manners to work. Boarding barns in particular require everyone to be on good behavior, since so many people are trying to use the same facilities, often at the same time.

Clean up after yourself and your horse. Even if you are running late for a group trail ride, take the extra minute to scoop up manure and sweep up hair and hoof trimmings. Especially if you have pulled your horse's mane, clean up the mass of hair on the floor. It's very unpleasant for the next rider along to have to stand her horse in your horse's mess. Sweep the remnants into a

*After you've prepared your horse for a ride by using fly spray and grooming him, clean up after yourself.*

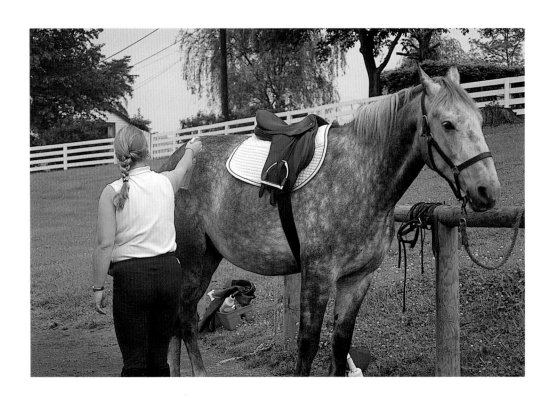

shovel, and get rid of them. If your horse urinated in the aisleway, find shavings to soak up the liquid, then remove the shavings.

Depending on the size of your barn, people may sometimes have to wait to use the cross-ties. If people need to get by you to reach other ties while your horse is using one set, unsnap your horse's halter on one side rather than simply lifting the rope. Also, keep your time in the cross-ties to a minimum so that others don't have to wait too long to use them.

Don't take other people's things without permission. You may have forgotten your safety stirrups, but if the owner of the pair you borrow needs hers, she will be in the same fix if you take them. Treat consumable horse items in the same way. Tail conditioner and horse treats should be left alone unless you ask permission first. Non-riding children pose a special problem at boarding and lesson barns. Major safety issues aside (little children easily get hurt in an environment with high haylofts and heavy equipment), others shouldn't have to watch your children, which they inevitably must if you let them run wild at the barn. Your dog should stay home too. It is hard to keep track of him while you are riding, and as with unattended children, dogs running loose can stress other riders.

In a boarding barn, try to keep your opinions to yourself as much as possible. Just as in an office or neighborhood situation, gossip is rude because it undermines community spirit, but in barns it gets particularly pernicious, because allegations tend to snowball rapidly where horses and their care are concerned. Express your feelings straight to barn management instead of to your friends.

## Ring Manners

If you have ever schooled your horse along with other competitors for a show, you know how hectic it can get when many people are trying to ride in a small space. In a ring, passing is left shoulder to left shoulder (the left as you are looking at the other horse). If you and another rider are going in the same direction, let the other rider know if you will be passing on the inside or the outside (next to the rail). Inside is the traditional way to go, but if it seems like the person will be circling or heading toward the inside of the ring, you may want to pass on the outside.

Monitoring speed—both yours and those riding with you—is an important part of riding in the ring. If you are the slowest one riding, and people are schooling their horses at the canter or lope on the rail, it is polite to stay inside to stay out of their way. If you are the one cantering, however, your main goal is to ride predictably so others can anticipate where you are going. Don't tailgate people who are going more slowly, and if you see that someone is new to riding or seems to be having trouble for some reason, stay away. She does not need your horse coming up behind her and scaring her horse.

Using a communal ring to jump in requires a different set of notifications. There's nothing worse than quietly trotting along and having a horse just over a three-foot wall come bearing down on you at full speed when neither of you have time to react properly. Tell other riders what your course is as it changes. You can just call out "liverpool to flowerbox," to give people a heads-up.

## Basic Trail Manners

"Multi-use" describes a trail that is not only a biking, hiking, or horse trail, but one that is to be shared. Some of the issues that arise on a trail like this have been covered in the last chapter, but a few additional rules of the road apply. Right-of-way is often important on a multi-use trail, and for the most part, people should yield to you. If you have ever spent any time sailing, you know that boats under motor power are always supposed to yield to sailboats, but this doesn't always happen. You have to use common sense. If a huge motorboat is bearing down on you, you get your sailboat out of the way, regardless of custom. It is the same with trail riding. Theoretically, cyclists should yield to you, pulling over to let you pass. But not everyone will do that, and it is better for you to hop off or pull your horse to the side so that the cyclist can tear by you. Otherwise you put yourself in a position where your horse might spook and cause a terrible—spiraling spokes, flying hooves—accident.

You will probably see some permutation of these manners posted at any park at which you ride. They all stem from basic consideration and common sense, and heeding them means a more pleasant experience for you and every other rider on the trail.

Particularly if you are riding with others, you owe it to everyone to know your mount well. If your horse causes trouble by bolting or spooking often, it will spoil your day, and can ruin theirs if they have to wait for you, chase you and your horse, or simply worry about you. If you happen to be on a horse you can't yet control, options are limited for the rest of the group. It's unsafe to send you home alone on a horse you're having trouble with, but it's also unsafe to keep going, since no one knows what the horse may do next. Rather than spoiling the ride for everyone,

Not all horses are ready to be ridden in a large group. Keep yourself safe by training your horse before you ride out with him.

wait to ride out until you know your horse well enough to control him, or have someone else ride him who is less concerned about controlling him while you start out on a more reliable and trustworthy mount.

Distance between horses is also key on the trail. They should always stay at least one horse's length away from one another, or about ten feet. If a horse decides to kick, wheel, or spook, distance creates a safety zone between him and the other horses.

Hand signals alert everyone on the ride to what the lead rider is planning. This rider is asking her group to wait behind her.

If your horse refuses a jump, go back to the end of the line before you try again. This may sound like a foxhunting formality, but it's not. Even if you are all stepping over a little log on the trail instead of jumping, or are even simply walking through a creek, if your horse won't take it the first time, go around the obstacle or go to the back of the group. It's not fair or polite to the other riders to hold them up, and watching your horse hesitate or refuse may make their horses reconsider an obstacle they had no trouble taking before.

When you are riding in a group that you are not leading, you must stay well behind the lead rider at all times, no matter how poky her horse is. She may use hand signals, like the basic hand out for slowing down, and may also turn to ask questions such as "Are we ready to trot?" That way, everyone moves together, and people are less likely to be caught unprepared. In a large ride, it is considerate to go at the pace of the least experienced rider in the group.

Polite riders stay off crops or planted land, where horses might ruin crops by trampling them or snacking on them. This is particularly important as so much space that was once rural becomes more suburban. With riding trails and areas harder to come by, it pays to be polite to the people who are allowing you to ride on their land.

When you get to a hill, look down to see if anyone is coming up. The riders on the way up have the right-of-way, since it is harder to keep a horse moving up than it is to keep one going down. The uphill riders should not have to stop their momentum by waiting for you coming down, especially on a narrow trail. Just pull up and wait for the uphill riders to pass you, then continue down and on your way.

Just as with the road, pass to the left and ride to the right. Try to stay at an even pace as you pass so that the other rider does not feel as if you are shooting by. Her horse may try to keep up with you, especially if you are both riding on your own, but will probably get bored with that pretty soon.

## Staying Safe

Once you've moved away from a basic walk on the trail, and you want to do a lot of cantering, you need to be sure you can control your horse. Horses, being herd animals, love to do what the other guy is doing. If you don't want to canter, but everyone else is cantering, chances are you will find yourself listening to that familiar three-beat rhythm before you even had a chance to pick up your reins. Stay in good communication with your riding buddies.

Pick your riding days with care. Almost all horses are more "up," or "hotter," when the weather is cool. Wind also adds to horses' edginess. They are more likely to run away, buck, and generally act up on a chilly and breezy day. You may want to lunge your horse before heading out if he seems too fresh to take out on the trail, or you may just want to wait for another day.

Don't head for home fast. Even if you're starting to run out of time, a walk or a controlled trot is the best way to get back to the barn. If you let your horse canter home, he is more likely to run away with you.

When you're riding on a narrow trail, your horse will sometimes give himself plenty of room to get by a tree or post, but your knee or foot will be too close. You end up kicking your foot out of the stirrup to avoid being smashed by the tree, which puts you in an unstable position. Instead, when you see something like this coming (which is not always a luxury you have), point your horse right toward the tree. He'll need to swing the rest of himself the other way, so you will have the clearance you need.

## Group Dynamics

As much as horses enjoy a trail ride to refresh their minds and bodies, they also feel intimidated by new surroundings. And each time you trail ride, there are potentially new things for your horse to see and hear. Being excitable does not necessarily mean he is misbehaving, but it means that he is uneasy. It's the rider's job to calm him down and keep him focused on the work ahead.

Giving him little jobs as you move along helps him "hear" you. This can be as simple as stopping and walking, again and again. Make circles, do leg yields, walk-trot transitions—anything to keep his mind on you. Especially once you start riding at speed on the trail, you need him to be listening to what you have to say. On the other hand, don't spend the whole ride making circles while the rest of the riders go by you, because your horse will, understandably, just become more and more undone as his buddies file by. He does not know that he won't be left.

Your horse is probably paying more attention to the horses

around him than he is to you, at least at the outset. If he is threatened by the horse in front of him, or his pasture buddy is all the way in the back of the line, he will be agitated.

When something fearsome arises, you don't have to let your horse sniff it. Even though that seems like it will entirely defuse his fear—and it may—it can also defeat your purpose since you want your horse to evaluate the object from the distance you want to pass at, and have him walk on by. If the scary object is on the move and is coming up behind you—a bicycle, a mule, a kayak— let your horse see it. Being prey animals, horses are particularly scared by things they cannot see.

Horses in a large group are attuned to their companions as well as their surroundings.

## Meeting Up

When you're riding solo, you may meet up with another rider by himself on the trail going in the same direction. Speak to her, just to say hello and let her know you're there. It's awkward to sort of trail along behind someone, and equally awkward to forge past in a cloud of dust. You should greet the person quietly, and ask if she is going the same way. If you want to ride together, ask if she minds and if her horse would prefer to lead or follow. If neither horse wants to follow, or if you're both riding solo because your horses don't like riding with others, just say so. You can also just trot on by until you're both riding alone again, but it is courteous to say that you're going to do so instead of just blowing by.

Should you be out for a quiet ride and be approached by someone else, speak up. Be polite, of course, but you don't have to let a stranger interrupt a trail ride you had counted on for some peace and quiet. You may have to alter your route, but should feel comfortable saying that today was just one of those days you'd hoped to spend alone with your horse. Most trail riders have had similar days, and will understand and leave you alone. Another day you might like some company.

## Time

If you have been riding for a while, you have probably noticed that horse people have a pretty loose sense of time—unless, of course, you're talking about seconds in a jump-off, or racing times. Otherwise, horse people tend to be late a lot, with horse shows and auctions often going late into the night, and trail rides mustering long before the last rider is ready to go as the earlier riders' horses whinny and stamp impatiently while everyone waits. I honestly don't know why this is, but it seems to be a real fact of life with horses and horse people.

This lack of timekeeping affects trail riding. It is annoying to be waiting for a lesson, and tiresome to wonder when the farrier will get there, but a whole day's plans come into play as far as time on the trail. The most agreeable way to ride is with no time constraints, so that you can ride as slowly as you like and choose new paths, but this is often impractical. You may be out with a group when someone spies an intriguing trail branching off from the main one. Everyone follows, and it is quite a while before the leader realizes that instead of a loop, she has just taken you way down an unmarked path miles from your original trail. Now you

Some days are
just made for
riding alone.

all have to turn around, adding an hour to your ride. On a fine day when you have nothing scheduled, this is what trail riding's all about—unexpected pleasures and enjoyment. But if your children are waiting to be picked up, or you are supposed to be meeting a client, you may be less than pleased that the event has taken a new and lengthening turn. It all seems like common courtesy, but somehow, getting near the horses and in the barn makes people instantly lose track of time.

Consideration dictates that you should be clear about time constraints when issuing or accepting an invitation. When that new trail is pointed out, just say that you'd like to check it out another time. Or simply offer to return to the barn alone. (This is a good reason to carry your own map and watch where you are, even if you are not in charge of the ride.)

If you're on the other side, and are offering to show people the new trail, ask if anyone has to get back to the barn. If everyone is game, keep on going. But if someone has to get back, particularly someone too inexperienced, overmounted, or unfa-

Talk to your trail companions to keep misunder-standings at bay and the day running smoothly. (The chestnut has a cloth in front of his muzzle to keep bugs away).

miliar with the area to find her own way back, it's best for everyone to save the adventure for another day, no matter how disappointing for the rest of the group.

Trailblazing is another time-consuming diversion that should be agreed to by everyone riding with you. Some people don't mind taking off through the woods without a marked trail, but many are uncomfortable with the practice, since it means branches in the face and inconsistent footing. It's also not good for the environment to blaze trails, since each new trail damages the existing terrain. (More on this in Chapter 8.) But if the situation is right, and you want to dive off through the woods, make sure everyone in the party wants to go and that no one feels pressured to add hours to their ride.

## Positioning

Trail riding in a group is like real estate in that it's all about location. Where you want your horse to be in a group is crucial to your enjoyment of the outing. If your best friend has a dominant horse who wants to be in the lead, and your horse is happier trailing along, you may have to find a different time to catch up with each other. Respecting where your horse wants to be and following a few basic rules will keep things safer and more fun for everyone. The ribbon system helps give other riders some sense of what is happening: a kicker gets a red ribbon in his tail, a green horse (or rider) can use a green ribbon, and a stallion should have a yellow ribbon in his tail. (Anyone riding a stallion in a group should be very confident of his calm nature and ability to be controlled around other horses.)

It's easy for a horse to get apprehensive on the trail, and the herd dynamics of the experience can add to this. Even if you are riding with a group of entirely new people and horses, your horse will still react to these dynamics as if he was out with a bunch of his pasturemates.

If your horse is a kicker, tradition demands that you tie a red ribbon in his tail so that others know to steer clear. But since all horses will kick in certain situations, and many people have been known to skip the ribbon, this old custom is not really enough. If your horse seems to be wheeling and making a lot of menacing faces, or baring his teeth, he may be about to kick. This is a good time to circle him or move him to the end of the line to distract him. In a shorter-term situation, turn him so that he is facing the other horse. If your horse is the victim of a horse bullying him, he may simply move away from instinct. But if you stay a safe distance away from the horse in front of you, your horse won't get kicked.

If your horse won't let you keep him at a safe distance, circle him as a way to remind him of what the task at hand is. If the horse he is clinging to is a pasturemate, he is probably looking for security. Still, riding up on another horse's rump is always unsafe, so keep working him until he settles a comfortable distance away. More saddle time at home and even more solo trail work will keep him tuned in to you instead of just the other horses.

Another problem that arises when out on the trail, especially with buddies, is a refusal to pass. First, see if the other horse is menacing to your horse, or if there is some questionable footing that your horse may be trying to avoid. He may have a perfectly good reason for staying put. If he doesn't, then ask him to go on,

Staying far enough behind the horse in front of you will prevent your horse from getting kicked.

**Everyday Trail Riding**

or at least to come up next to the other horse. If your horse is the opposite, and just wants to lead, let him if at all possible. Just keep paying attention to your riding so it's not all his idea.

## When You're Up Front

On bigger trail rides, it's a good idea to have both lead and drag riders. The lead rider, obviously, is the person in front, while the drag rider stays behind. It's bad form for other riders either to pass the lead rider or to fall behind the drag rider. Keeping the same riders lets people know who is making decisions. On a very large ride, someone closer to the back can take a problem to the drag rider. It is the lead rider's job to decide when the trail ride moves forward, and if everyone needs to stop, and to carry a halter and lead rope in case she needs to pony another horse.

Being the lead horse and rider has some responsibilities. You tend to see things first (as well as get the most spiderwebs in your face). As you see changes in the trail and footing, advise those following you through your actions. Rotten logs, patches of mud, holes, low branches—these are all your responsibility to warn the other riders about. If you're in deep woods, keep people far enough apart so that they don't thwack each other in the face with branches. Keep your horse from hurrying up or down hills so that others don't follow suit.

You have to be a bit of diplomat, too, and keep speed to something that suits all the riders. Let people know you want to trot, or canter, and make sure they are doing all right once you get going. You can use bicycle riders' hand signals to "tell" people behind you what is going on. An arm extended with the hand pointing down means slow. Some people like to wait until this signal gets to the back of the pack to lessen the chance of horses running up on top of each other's rear ends. Others, however, let the leader slow down first and then allow the effect to trickle back, which only works if everyone is following safely. Decide which works for your group before you leave the barn. For the most part, stick to walking and trotting in a big group. Foxhunters are used to group galloping, but the rest of us are often courting danger by deciding to ride at speed in a herd situation.

If you decide to organize trail rides for friends or children, you will need to be insured and briefed on equestrian law. Like a boarding barn, you will need signed release forms, and to insist upon helmets for everyone. (Running paying trail rides is something beyond the scope of this book. However, if you plan to charge for trail rides, make sure you have a lawyer help you with release forms and have plenty of experienced help on the rides themselves.)

Watch people ride in a ring before getting out on the trail with them. Even people who insist that they are good riders bear watching, since they may be remembering back to some lessons at a summer camp many years ago, or a few pasture rides on a friend's horse.

Whenever you are leading a group, especially a group of new or even first-time riders, have an emergency plan, and ride areas that you know very well. This way, if you have to call for help, you will be able to tell the ambulance exactly where you are. It is a good idea to get certified in CPR and first aid if you plan to lead many rides. And don't forget a first aid kit for riders as well as for horses.

Even in a situation with a few friends, where the trail ride is not particularly organized and thus does not have a "lead rider" as such, you may find yourself in charge simply because of your position. Often, your horse will decide whether you are going to be the lead rider or if you'll be in back of the pack (which may mean he's only behind one other horse). Many horses have marked preferences about how they like to travel on the trail when they are out with others. But if your horse does not seem to mind leading or following (or if you'd like to teach him to accept both positions), you should offer to alternate with others on the ride.

If you're in the lead, and need to talk to the other people riding with you, turn around in your saddle to address them. It's very difficult to hear someone who is talking to the trees up ahead, and frustrating to hear sound coming out but only see the person's back.

# Children

Children on foot pose a special problem for trail riders, even though they, of all pedestrians, are usually the happiest to see riders. Most children find horses exciting, and will hope for an opportunity to pat your horse and speak with you. As soon as you spot a child on the trail, slow down to a walk, as children (even those who have their own ponies) are notorious for darting out in front of horses and spooking them. Say hello, but don't feel you have to stop if you don't want to. It is very nice to allow your horse to be patted, and provides an opportunity for you to teach the children a bit about horses—"Pat his neck or shoulder, not too hard," and so on—but you are, of course, under no obligation to do so.

Some children are frightened by horses. After all, they are so very much bigger than children, and children unfamiliar with them may be scared of their hooves or teeth. If a child seems frightened to you, wait for her parents to collect her, and then ask

Many children love seeing and patting horses, so if you can, allow them some time with yours.

if you can pass by. If the parent seems to want to acclimate the child to horses, decide if you are comfortable with your horse acting as an object lesson. If this is all right with you, simply talk to both parent and child as they examine your horse. If you'd prefer to keep riding, or just don't think your horse will appreciate this kind of attention, apologize and politely tell the parent that you need to keep going.

Groups of children almost always necessitate dismounting, just because they are so unpredictable. When you come across a school or camp field trip on your shared equestrian trail, you can pretty much figure that you will have to get off, as someone is likely to dash over to you, or at the very least, shout and scare your horse.

Riding along with children also requires another set of manners. Children can be wonderful riding teachers for adults because of their natural fearlessness. They will jump things that look too high for their ponies without giving them a second glance, and gallop in an open field without thinking about it. On the other hand, children can be tough trail partners because they don't have a very good sense of time or space, so they often will ask to go back to the barn when you are miles away from it, or plead to stay out longer only to realize, half an hour later, that they are hot and thirsty and want to go home. So know your children and their riding levels. Take them trail riding with a patient and understanding buddy unless the others on the ride are also parents, and preferably also accompanied by kids. No matter how talented a rider your child is, she's still a child, and you should make some of the decisions. If a well-meaning lead rider asks your child if she'd like to jump a large log, and you know it's too much for her or her horse, speak up. Everyone would rather have a seemingly pushy parent than a bad accident on the trail.

You can help your child and her pony by doing some of the training on the pony yourself. Accustom the pony to branches and other hazards of the trail (more on this in Chapter 2). But also do things that children do—mount and dismount from each side, shout, drop the reins—and anything else you imagine your child will do when she is riding him. A set of anti-grazing reins may be a nice gift for a child whose pony loves to eat while being ridden out. And a child's horse, whether he is a pony or not, should learn to be "ponied," so that you can always lead him from your horse if your child gets frightened or tired.

Also, avoid taking neophyte children trail riding. When your friend from work tells you how much her daughter loves horses, issue an invitation to ride in the ring or the field near the barn first. A beginner child may seem eager and game at the outset of a trail ride, but may get increasingly exhausted and frightened as the day goes on. Save the trail ride invitations for children you know. Trail rides make wonderful treats for children who are used to riding lessons in an arena, day in and day out.

## Water

We all know the proverb about leading a horse to water. Many horses are finicky about drinking water away from home, but most trail riders will want their horses to stop and take advantage of a creek or stream that crosses or follows the trail. Dehydration is a common problem in trail horses, so watering becomes a crucial part of the day and ride. As you approach people at a watering

Narrow, leafy trails mean everyone should be careful of branches at eye level.

spot, make sure their horses have drunk before you ride off. Horses will want to follow a horse leaving, and it's rude to create a situation where a horse who has not yet had any water will follow yours, especially when the rider wants the horse to drink.

## Smoking

If you smoke, you have heard all about its detrimental effects and know by now the many reasons that it is a bad idea for you and those around you. But smoking on horseback is particularly bad because it's dangerous to be concentrating on something other than your riding. Also, cigarette butts can easily start forest fires. You should really extinguish your cigarette and then "pack out" the butt with the rest of your trash.

## Urinating Horse

To show consideration for your horse when he is urinating, stand up in your stirrups. Although horses can defecate while they are walking, horses need to stop to urinate. They give you plenty of notice when they need to go; they "park out" and stretch with their front legs far forward and their hind legs far back. When you stand, you take some weight off his back and let him stretch more easily. It is a nice thing to do for your horse.

Some old-timers say that sitting in the saddle when a horse is urinating will hurt his kidneys. As tenaciously as this belief is held, it's really not so. There is just too much padding between you and a horse's kidneys, and they are well behind the saddle area. If you were to slam or press down on your horse's back while he was urinating, however, it might cause some pain.

## Mountain Bikes

Mountain bikers (for our purposes, anyone who rides his or her bicycle on dirt and hills instead of in the road) and riders often have a slightly antagonistic relationship. For so many years, horse-back riders got full claim to the trails wending through national parks. When mountain biking became popular, though, bridle paths presented themselves as the most appropriate places to ride a mountain bike, especially in an urban park. Equestrians were unhappy about the mountain bikes they met whizzing by them on their formerly quiet trails.

As trails and open space in general become harder and harder to find, it behooves equestrians to make peace with mountain bikers. Some mountain bikers feel that because of their greater numbers, they should "own" the paths, and equestrians should make way. Meanwhile, some riders believe that they were here first, and the mountain bikers should respect us and our enormous, but easily scared by strange machines, mounts. Because we have more in common than not, however, riders and mountain bikers should band together to save space rather than being at odds with one another. The best long-term solution to mountain bikers on your trail is acclimating your horses to them through repeated exposure and training at home.

Dirt bikes, even more than mountain bikes, can cause horses to spook. Dirt bikes are the motorized mini-motorcycles that can go on varied terrain, so in areas where they are popular, you are likely to encounter them on a bridle path. As if the motor itself were not enough to convince your horse he is facing a monster, some dirt bike riders wear loud-colored outfits and helmets that conceal their faces, causing your terrified horse to imagine he is being hunted by a hot-pink and chartreuse inhuman creature.

Since trail sharing is the way of the future, your job is to make your horse learn to pass scary objects. He does not need to stand around and watch a dirt bike endlessly, but he does need to pass one without spooking or bolting. With any of these vehicles, keep your horse's head toward them. If your horse hears a bicycle or other spooker behind him, he will think he is being pursued and be more likely to bolt. While people used to think that the key was to keep horses away from things like dirt bikes, which, to an equestrian eye, seem designed particularly effectively in order to scare horses, it now seems that it's our responsibility as horse people to acclimate our horses to these vehicles. After moving to an area where I share the trail I ride the most with many bicyclists, I've gotten used to them, and so has Romeo, for the most part. It took quite a bit of time before I stopped tensing up every time I heard wheels behind me, but once I did, Romeo became calmer too.

## Boats

Obviously, many riders don't have to worry about boats. But if you ride along a lake, river, or canal, you may see some watercraft as you go. Water is already somewhat foreign to most horses, and boats (and swimmers) can often frighten them even more. One way to help your horse is to be sure that he knows that the strange craft is moving on water. Bobbing buoys, the glinting of aluminum paddles, and the strange silhouettes of kayak helmets can also be scary. Have him inspect the lake or riverbank, and then judge the situation again. You may need to get off the first few times, but after a while, your horse should get used to boats, just as he will to other spooky objects. And as with bicycles or baby carriages, boats have people speaking around them. Many horses calm down once they realize that something foreign is just another crazy scheme dreamed up by humans.

One thing that makes Romeo absolutely terrified, no matter how many he sees it, is people portaging a canoe. We often ride along a canal with a towpath, which used to be for the mules who pulled the canal boats. He has gotten better about the canoes and kayaks themselves, but when he sees them stop and sprout legs to cross the towpath, I am usually found on the ground, holding the reins as I try to explain to the kind and curious canoers why my horse is doing his best Black Stallion imitation.

## Branches

When trail riding in the woods, you are often in a snug single file with other riders. You should all be at least one horse's length apart from each other as you ride. If you encounter a low-hanging

branch, just duck under it. If you try to hold it, it could snap back and hit the next rider in the face. If the branch seems to have a life of its own and swatted you in the face, call "Ware branch!" to the next person in line. "Ware" comes from "beware," and is used by foxhunters. Anything you see to which you want to alert others can be prefaced by a "ware." "Ware barbed wire," "Ware deer," and so on.

This group is keeping their horses quietly at a creek to give them the opportunity to drink.

## Puddles

Even horses who willingly cross streams don't like puddles. Romeo is like this—he just doesn't like anything that splashes too much. After much time and work spent near puddles and water, he will cross them when I ask, but whether he is in the arena or out on the trail, he steps very gingerly through anything vaguely resembling a puddle.

Horses don't know, as we do, that puddles are shallow and

safe to cross. Ask your horse to go forward, but also let him pick his spot from which to evaluate the situation. Don't let him duck away, but give him a minute to size things up. He might even want to paw the puddle, which is fine unless you think he is about to roll. Once you get your horse across a puddle the first time, let him come back and forth repeatedly until it seems routine.

## When a Horse Gets Loose

You have probably been at a show and heard the call "Loose horse!" rise through the crowd. It seems as if at least one horse has to get out at every show, whether he has jerked away from a rider who wasn't paying attention, or dumped his rider and headed back for his trailer. On the trail, a horse usually gets loose if someone drops her reins while she's dismounted to open or close a gate, or if a horse spooks and deposits his rider on the ground.

If you are alone and your horse is loose, all you can do is what you would do if he were refusing to be caught in the field: feign indifference. If you don't challenge a horse, but look as if you did not have a care in the world, he will usually come up to you.

If you're in a group and a horse gets loose, if everyone else is still mounted, he probably won't go too far. He may bolt, but will want to stay near the other horses. Give him a minute and he should return. If he starts to play the can't-catch-me game, have everyone move off slowly and more than likely he will be eager enough to stay with his buddies that he will become easy to catch.

## Organized Trail Rides

An "organized trail ride" means a ride more organized than even a sign-up sheet at a boarding barn asking "Who's up for the loop on Saturday?" Instead, organized trail rides often end up with the largest groups with people of all ages and experience riding together. They are often sponsored by breed associations or regional organizations. Riders muster together, and set out over a day or weekend on the same trail. It's a great way for people to find riding companions, and to enjoy a ride that may also include cookouts, camping, and other social events. Some group trail rides even have a wagon train and feature historical reenactments.

Each ride will have its own rules, which each rider should heed. Group dynamics become very important in an organized trail ride, which can have hundreds of riders. You will probably be required to have proof of a negative Coggins test before you bring your horse into contact with so many others.

## Commercial Trail Rides

Encountering a group of people on a commercial trail ride can be a bit tough for the experienced rider. You're meeting up with a group of people who are likely to be new riders; some of them are probably experiencing their first ride. The horses, on the other hand, have been on the same path so many times that they are not really paying attention, but plodding along, nose to tail. Even though this may slow your own ride down, be alert and helpful if you can. Use care when passing so that you don't alarm any of the horses, and be kind. These people will remember their ride, and your politeness may be the kind of thing that turns them into more serious riders.

If you are away from home and decide to take one of these trail rides, enjoy the scenery. Be sure that your girth is tightened before you set out, because with all the work the trail leaders have to do, they may not have a chance to adjust all the tack before each ride. Ask to ride near whomever you came with, since part of the fun of these rides is seeing the park with a companion.

Don't assume that just because a horse works in a trail string, he is a poky automaton. On one commercial trail ride I went on, the tour was conducted on tapes inside a Walkman. (The safety of this is questionable, but the tour leaders seemed used to it.) I made the mistake of admitting I had ridden before when the tour leaders asked, and wound up on one of their newer horses while my husband got a placid mule. Eventually, I dropped my headphones, which hit the horse I was riding in the shoulder, which made her spook on pavement and skid around as I tried to pick up the bouncing headphones, which were dangling from a wire. Everything turned out fine, but I learned quickly that even a commercial trail horse is still a horse.

# Preparing for Outdoor Riding

6

Between weather, natural obstacles, and your horse, there are many variables involved in every trail ride. Knowing how to deal with changing seasons and terrain means more time spent on favorite trails and more time exploring new ones. When you understand the outdoors and appreciate its diversity, you become a more self-sufficient and game trail rider.

## Cold Weather Riding

No one really knows what revs horses up in the wintertime, but just when you are feeling snuggly and ready for slow-moving work, your horse is frisky. Why this is so is something of a mystery. One explanation may be that it's not that winter is easy on horses so much as that summer is tough—with the flies and pollen floating around, horses have a hard time in the heat. In the winter, though, their coats keep them warm, the air is clear, and they generally feel much better than we do.

129

When winter hits, having horses provides you with a new list of activities, like blanketing, breaking ice in troughs, hauling hay and warming bran mash. Sometimes these tasks get so overwhelming that riding, the reason you got these horses in the first place, gets lost in the shuffle. The cold weather can definitely make riding more challenging than during the spring or summer, but with some preparation and equipment changes, you and your horse can enjoy the winter as much as you do the other times of the year.

Riders accustomed to conditions in an indoor arena in the cold need to be attuned to ground conditions if they decide to head out on the trail. Snow is no reason to stay in. Frozen grass can be very slippery, and long hours of riding on solidly frozen packed dirt can be hard on a horse's legs and feet, but a little bit of snow can provide more traction than the frozen, ice-slick ground. Jumping is often strictly curtailed or even cancelled if there is snow on the ground. If it's icy or slick, ride straight up hills, because riding at an angle up an incline can make it easier for the horse to slip and fall.

Riding in snow is a beautiful experience, with the frosted trees and the muffled sounds of the horses' hooves. Snow somewhat mitigates the surface of the ground although it can be tricky to ride in. Shoeing with special shoes—whether snow pads, or ice calks (shoes with protruding metal)—can help if you plan to do a lot of winter riding. Borium (a brand name for the mineral tungsten carbide) also helps traction.

If the snow is deep, it can make your horse sore to move through it. Powder is the best, but be alert for ice beneath from an earlier storm. Snow that is crusty can be dangerous, because the icy crust can cut your horse's legs when he sinks through it.

Icy spots are terrifying to horses for good reason. You should be wary of them too. Horses can slip and slide on ice just as we can, but once they have lost their balance and fall, they may be unable to get back up. You can put de-icing chemicals on icy spots of a well-used trail, or at least mark it somehow so other riders know to avoid it.

# Winter Shoeing

Many riders modify their horse's shoes during the winter. If you just trail ride occasionally or gently outdoors during the winter, your horse may be able to stick with his regular shoeing or even go barefoot. For sporadic riding, you can sometimes get away with quick fix-its, like cooking spray or petroleum jelly on your horse's hooves to repel packed snow. But for serious outdoor riding, many trail riders take a lesson from eventers and show jumpers and consider studs, at least on their horse's rear shoes.

Traction shoeing, which is shoeing with calks, Borium, or other friction-causing devices, helps horses' hooves grip the ground better. Just like soccer cleats or golf shoes, these are athletic devices. For an all-weather and all-season trail horse, traction assistants may be a godsend for the rider who wants to give her horse some help on a slick or icy surface. Traction shoeing is not for every horse, especially one with joint or muscle problems. You may find that calks, for example, increase stress on his already weakened areas. In fact, most of us really don't need additions to our horse's shoes, as long as we have good, regular farrier work.

Ask your farrier what traction devices are best for your horse. Here are (left to right) shoes with snow pads, Borium, and calks. (McGraw photo)

But if you trail ride every day, or in many challenging conditions, your shoer may recommend one of the following options, which are only a few among many possibilities in a complex world of farriery that gets more advanced and technologically savvier every year.

Like calks, studs (which screw onto the shoe) help horses gain purchase on icy or slick surfaces. For trail riders, calks are nice because they are cheaper and simpler—the farrier puts them on and you're done—but studs give you the advantage of customizing. When you want to use the studs, you can, but when you prefer not to have any studs on your shoes, you're not committed to an advanced level of traction the way you would be with calks. To further complicate things, studs come in different sizes, so you can use smaller ones for a grassy wet field and larger ones for ice, but most trail riders will stick with one medium-sized set for icy days in particular.

Most horses wear prefabricated, or "keg," shoes. Basic kegs have a groove along the side that collects dirt and provides rudimentary traction. Some shoes are fullered (grooves have straight sides), and some are swedged (grooves have slanted sides), and there are all kinds of in-betweens as well. Rimmed shoes have rims on the inner or outer edge of the shoe that give the shoe more opportunity for traction by grabbing the dirt. (A harness racer has high rims on the outside, for example, to help him gain purchase on the hard track.)

The mineral tungsten carbide is often called Borium by horse people, since that is the trade name for the mineral wrapped in steel that is used to increase traction for horses. Some people have their farriers apply Borium to the toe and heel regions of the shoes, although it can also be spread more evenly on the shoes. While commonly used for traction in wintertime, Borium can also be useful on a horse who is consistently ridden over rocks and gravel.

If you don't want to commit to Borium all over your horse's shoes, consider asking your farrier about Borium nails, which won't affect the horse's way of going in the same way that Borium on the shoe can. Thicker dollops of Borium act basically like calks. The farrier melts the Borium with a torch or on her forge and

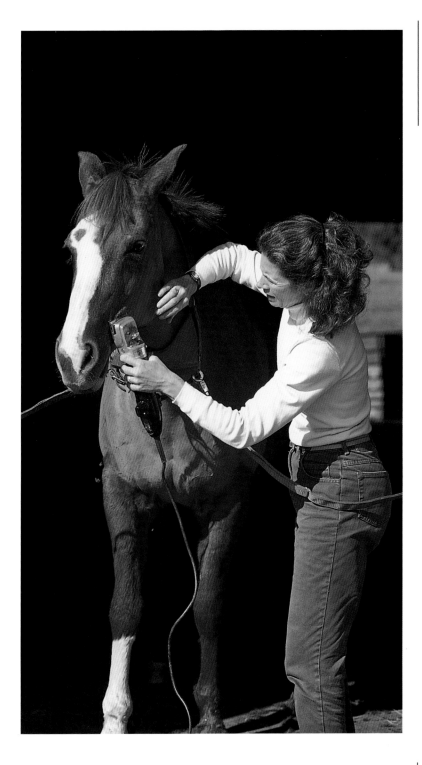

Clipping kept to a minimum will keep your trail horse warm during the winter months.

applies it on the shoe to an ⅛– to ¼–inch thickness. Ask your farrier if you think any of these options could help you and your horse have some safer rides, particularly in the winter.

## Horse Clothing

Like shoeing, horse clothing can help your winter trail riding go more smoothly. Much depends, of course, on how your horse is kept—obviously, a furry pasture horse's main difficulty may be cooling down after working instead of warming up. Even if you do not blanket regularly, you may need some kind of rug to throw over your pasture horse until he cools down and dries off. Because this process can take so long, many people opt for a trace clip, which keeps the chest short but leaves a winter-length coat all over the rest of the horse's body.

Quarter sheets can really assist the body-clipped or hunter-clipped horse. Having one available for your clipped horse can mean you can school outside on a chillier day than you could otherwise. Don't try to bunch your regular cooler up under the saddle to form a quarter sheet, because the extra straps and fabric will make this not only cumbersome but also dangerous as well.

## Rider's Clothes

To maintain the range of motion you need to ride but still keep warm, look for clothes that offer minimal bulk with maximum warmth. Breeches and riding tights now come in Polarfleece® and other warm synthetic fabrics, and with some long underwear beneath these breeches, you will be very warm.

If you don't see what you want in tack stores, check out sports stores. They stock a good selection of close-fitting, warm long underwear, especially in silk and its synthetic equivalents. Many heavy riding jackets are cut with side flaps to cover your saddle as well as your back, but many riders opt for vests, which allow for more movement and more layering. Try layering silk or other minimally bulky long underwear with close-fitting shirts and a fleece jacket or shirt. A windproof anorak on top of all this will help protect you from the wind and keep you warmer.

Feet get particularly cold on a winter ride. If you live in an area that is consistently freezing, consider investing in boots with warm liners and insulation. Some riders find the type of battery-powered or self-generating boot warmers that skiers, hikers, and field hunters use helpful as they are small and can create heat for a few hours. You can also buy these battery-powered warmers for the pockets of your coat. If you live in a climate where the winters are mild, you can often use layers of socks (silk ones as the first layer work well) and ride in looser-fitting boots, like old paddock boots that may have loosened a bit, Blundstones or even duck boots to accommodate the extra bulk of the sock layers. Since you will be riding gently in the winter anyway, the extra padding should not be too much of a problem.

Gloves are essential. Look for a pair with flexibility as well as warmth, so that you can hold the reins well. With gloves, you may want to buy something made expressly for riding, as gloves for other winter sports often do not allow for the range of motion you need. Some Polarfleece gloves have suede on the ring and index fingers, and other gloves have three fingers, so that you have the warmth of a mitten with a place to hold the reins.

Be creative and look to gear and clothing intended for other winter sports to suit your needs. Ski gear often comes in handy, for example. To keep your ears warm under your helmet, consider a knitted or fleece headband, or earmuffs if you think a band might be too bulky. Knit collars that cover nose, mouth, and neck can protect you from the wind when you ride. Tack shops have helmet covers that go over your entire helmet, and fasten under your chin, covering your head and ears, but any close-fitting ear warmer will work well.

## Summer Riding: Heat and Thunderstorms

When it's very hot outside, your horse will struggle more than he does in bitter cold. While you may prefer a lazy trail ride on a summer afternoon, he will find it hard to work when the temper-

Allowing your horse to drink plenty of water minimizes the risk of dehydration.

ature gets up into the 80s, 90s, or beyond. Breed and conformation have something to do with the ability to withstand heat: a pudgy Quarter Horse will have more trouble than a fit Arabian, for example, in summer. But heat takes its toll on all horses.

When you are trail riding in hot weather, help your horse by allowing him all the water he wants beforehand. Grass, which is so full of water, is good as well. And keep him off the grain for at least four or five hours before you saddle up. As you ride, be alert to signs of heat exhaustion or stroke (see Chapter 7), and dehydration.

Heat exhaustion is a mild form of heatstroke. Your exhausted horse may sweat excessively, and at the worst, collapse. If your horse starts showing fatigue on a hot day, stop riding and cool him off with water, shade, and fans if you are close to the barn. If he does not improve, you may need to call the vet, because your horse may be verging on heatstroke, a severe and dangerous condition worse than heat exhaustion.

You can tell if your horse is becoming dehydrated by pinching some of his skin. It should bounce right back when you release it. If it doesn't, he may be losing fluid. Stop riding, and give him water. Summertime sweating can lead to the loss of electrolytes as well as water, but don't overdo it on the electrolyte supplements. As long as your horse has free-choice salt, he should have enough in his diet. That should help keep him from dehydrating. The most general rule is that a horse should drink one gallon of water for each hundred pounds of body weight. Satisfying this need can be a problem if you have a field-boarded horse who drinks from a trough with other horses.

Take advantage of the shade. Walk when the trail is shaded, and pick up a little trot in the sun. And don't believe the "too much water" myth. Letting your thirsty and hot horse drink will not make him founder. He may get some stomach cramps, however, so it is better to walk him to cool him down and let him drink small amounts of water as he goes. Hose him down, too. Keep scraping him with a sweat scraper as you allow the water to run over him, because extra water on his skin will just heat up and act as insulation, the opposite of what you are trying to achieve.

Summer also brings heavy thunderstorms. Major storms can

A shady trail—perfect for a cool summer ride.

change the terrain you're riding. A heavy rain makes riding trails very slippery. If you decide to stay mounted when it gets that slick, avoid trails with no vegetation when you can. Watch local creeks or rivers for dramatic changes, too, for they can swell rapidly.

Take cover if you see lightning. Don't wait until the rain is actually pouring on top of you and your horse. You should be able to hear thunder up to ten miles away. Remember the old counting method to determine the proximity of a storm. When you can count five seconds ("one Mississippi, two Mississippi. . .") in between seeing the lightning and hearing the thunder, it's only a mile away. Counting to "ten Mississippi" means that the storm is two miles away and so on.

Lightning seeks the easiest way to get to the ground. This is why you avoid trees; the lightning may try to go from the tree through you in an effort to get to the ground. This is why a building—or even a shed—offers better shelter. (Just don't touch the walls, or anything else that is wet or metal.) This is why lightning rods are a good idea on barns—they get the lightning straight into the ground instead of allowing the building to hold the charge until someone comes along to ground it.

If you are caught in the open, get away from your horse. Tie or ground-tie him or even turn him loose, since horses wearing metal shoes are more likely to get hit than you are. You want as little of you to touch the ground as possible, so crouch down. Chances are you will not get hit, but it's best to be safe, and stay crouched until the storm is over.

## Mud

If you know the trails are likely to be muddy, put bell boots on your horse before you go out, since bells help stop your horse from overreaching and grabbing his front heel. Stay away from any area that looks swampy, but if you have to dip into a swamp, let your horse choose his own way with plenty of rein. Horses can get panicky once they sink up to their hocks, because they struggle so much to move by then that they are truly stuck. If your horse is having trouble moving, consider dismounting so he does not have to free your weight too.

Bell boots prevent a horse's rear toes from grabbing and hurting his front heels in muddy conditions.

Try to avoid muddy or boggy footing whenever you can. Standing water is a likely spot for bogs, and sometimes a swampy area can be found right in the middle of what looks like a grassy plain. Horses have an uncanny way of knowing if the footing is unsafe, so pay attention if your horse is acting odd about a certain spot. You can always dismount and use a long stick to check yourself if you feel unsure. Allowing your horse to get mired can result in a rescue operation or his getting hurt.

## Water

Water is always a problem on the trail, either because there is too little water, and the horses are thirsty, or because there is too much and everything is flooded and sloppy. Horses need drinking water all the time, and as they work along a trail, their needs increase. Some parks provide troughs with municipal or well water, but usually when you're on the trail, you're faced with natural sources, such as rivers or ponds. The water you encounter on the trail is not likely to be pure. No water really is. Water can be contaminated, and your horse may tell you by refusing to drink it, or stopping mid-swallow. If it smells bad, keep your horse moving.

Water that has been contaminated by bacteria borne by feces can harm your horse. Usually, you would be worse off than he would if you drank it, but aged or very young or sick horses can be harmed by fecally contaminated water. Stay abreast of local health concerns. If there has been some kind of wildlife disease outbreak where you ordinarily ride, don't let your horse drink from local creeks.

Ponds are particularly likely to be unsafe for horses. In fact, they are sometimes fenced off. Blue-green algae, which thrives in ponds, can poison horses. It can cause diarrhea, and in severe cases, even convulsions and death. This algae grows best in summer and fall, and loves stagnant, shallow water. If you have a pond on your own property, have a water treatment company sample the water. There are remedies, from stocking the pond with fish who love eating algae to draining or cleaning out the pond once in a while.

# Swimming

Fording a stream or low creek is not too big a deal. Many horses don't like to cross water, but unless the rocks are extremely slippery or sharp, most horses can cross low water with ease, even up to knee or hock level. They may not love it, but as long as you are determinedly looking ahead, they will tend to go, especially if trail buddies are heading on. If your horse starts to paw and blow into the water, urge him on—he may be considering a roll or lying down.

Once the water starts coming up to your horse's shoulder, he may want to swim. This is only fun if you are used to it and have swum a horse quite a bit. If you've never swum a horse, it can be a bit unnerving. It is a totally new sensation even for someone who has logged many miles on horseback. Horses are good swimmers, though, so even on your first venture, you will probably be just fine.

Always be very careful when fording, since many bottom

When a horse starts to paw in the water, he may be considering a roll.

areas can be soft and have deep holes. If you're in a park, ask rangers where it's best to cross. As your horse goes from walking to swimming, you will feel him surging forward in small increments. As this happens, kick your feet out of the stirrups. Keep your reins in your hand so that they don't get caught in his legs and accidentally tangled up.

Stay upstream of your horse. This means that if you are crossing a river in which the water flows north to south, you should be leaning north. That way, if something happens and the horse gets knocked out from under you, he won't hit or tumble over you on the way down. If you get scared or become uneasy, push off that way as well. Let him find his way to the riverbank. As soon as you feel him walking again, get your stirrups back and pick up your reins.

If you're really lucky, you will get to ride in the ocean some day. This is not for beginners—equine or human. On a hired horse who is used to the ocean, this will be easy. The people in the glossy ads for Caribbean travel are not riding bareback just for the romance of it—bareback is actually a great way to ride in the ocean, since it saves your saddle from getting totally soaked. You may want to shed your boots for the same reason, and grab mane instead of pulling on the reins and possibly getting tangled and dragged under. A horse who is new to it may take some dismounted time to get accustomed to the idea, and a day with big waves crashing is never a good day for a ride in the surf. The first few times that your horse experiences a wave taking his footing away, guide him back toward the beach so that he knows how he can get out. Things to watch for in the ocean, just as in any water, include mats of seaweed and underwater rocks. Watch for sandbars that will drop off and leave your horse pedaling madly where he thought there was footing.

## Desert Trail Riding

Desert riding is not for beginners—equine or human, either. Your horse needs to be in good shape to ride in the desert, or he can fall prey to heat exhaustion, dehydration, and colic. Deep sand, hills, and shoe-loosening rocks are all common. In deep sand, keep your horse to a walk.

Pack emergency water if you're riding in the desert, since depending on trail sources is risky. People need at least one gallon a day, and horses need at least ten gallons. Many desert riders also pack electrolytes. You can start giving them to your horse in the weeks before your desert ride; check with your vet to see when to begin. Ask local authorities if any desert springs or municipal or park water sources are up and running. If the one you were planning on happens to be dry, you'll need more water. Be aware that some desert parks ask that you have your horse drink at least 100 feet away from a natural water source, so you'll need to pack a collapsible feed pan.

Cactus can be a real problem. The thorns will hurt your horse if he brushes against them, and if you get thrown, you could land in yet more. Stick to the trails, and you probably won't encounter any cactus, but you may if you do some cross-country riding. It's a good idea to pack a fine-toothed comb, as the desert endurance riders do, to remove any cactus thorns.

Rattlesnakes are most active in the spring and the summer, and bites are usually on the horse's legs or face, which can swell dramatically. If your horse does get bitten, try to stay calm and lead him back to help. Many people ride in both bell boots and splint boots to guard a horse's legs against rattlesnake bites. If you ride in snake country often, you should keep two small pieces of hose with you. These can go into your horse's nostrils to keep him breathing in the case of a bite to the nose. It's not the venom itself that will harm him as much as being unable to breathe through swollen nasal passages. (See Chapter 7 for more on snakebites.)

## Hills

If you spend a lot of time riding steep (or even steepish) hills, there are ways to make the ascents and descents easier on your horse. Of course, the largest factor is your riding. If you and your horse are generally in harmony and balance with each other, even the steepest hill will not be a problem. If you're still a bit rough or learning or unbalanced, hills will be tough.

Some endurance riders do what is called "tailing" their horses. This means that the horse basically pulls you up a steep hill as you hold onto his tail. (Your horse needs to be the sort of trustworthy individual who doesn't mind having you behind him.)

Don't let your horse gain speed as he travels downhill, because he will just have that much more trouble stopping once he reaches the bottom. On a steep hill, stay straight, so that if your horse happens to slip, he'll just "sit down" instead of sliding all the way down the hill. Don't lean back, but stay tall in the saddle with your legs firmly under you. Just don't pull on the reins—he needs his head for balance. Riding downhill adds another reason that riding your horse's "rear engine" instead of guiding his head is important, as your work in any discipline from dressage to cutting will have taught you. Having a responsive horse helps on hill work as well, because if you feel him gaining too much momentum as he goes downhill, you need to be able to

Trust your horse to figure out the safest way to descend a hill. This horse is well-balanced and finding his own path down.

ask him to gather himself and stop (perform a half-halt, in other words) so that you can continue down safely and comfortably.

Downhill is one place where it is almost always best to stay on horseback. Hopping off is a good quick and safe way to handle a problem most of the time, but when you're going down a hill, it's best not to have a horse right behind you, because if he stumbles or trips he will be on top of you. Stay mounted and concentrate on keeping him together.

If there is another hill coming right up after the one you're on, you may want to let your horse speed up at the end to "coast" up the next hill if it is gentle and not steep. Come to a walk or a slow trot to balance yourself before heading up the next hill. (If it's steep, it will be too hard on him, and he may just try to jump the space between hills.) Also, stay on your horse's back on a steep slope. Sometimes it may be tempting to hop off, but then you're in danger of his slipping back and falling on you.

If he's fatigued, don't have him go straight down a gently sloping hill. Instead, let him tack or zigzag back and forth across it to put less stress on him. Trotting down steeper hills is best left to really balanced pairs, because you want to maintain contact with his mouth the whole time. Taking a few steps backward as your horse goes down a hill is a good strengthening exercise. In any case, you should do a lot of half-halts and balancing as you go down a steep hill. Going downhill is hard work for horses, so yours may balk as he goes down. Keep him moving, but also keep him balancing.

Going uphill, your horse may want to speed up. Try to ask him to engage his hindquarters and stay at a calm pace. This is better for his muscles and gets him out of the habit of plunging up the slightest incline. The goal is to keep his hindquarters propelling him forward. Also, don't be afraid to grab some mane if it will keep you from grabbing him in the mouth.

## Jumping

Jumping on the trail can be very enjoyable. If you're used to jumping in a ring, you will now see what all those arena jumps are

Anything—like
these low logs—
can be a fun jump
out on the trail.

painted to resemble, and get to jump the real thing. Real logs, streams, and stone walls are waiting. Just remember that these do not have any safety mechanisms. They don't fall down if touched, and the other side is not necessarily on good footing. Inspect anything you intend to jump before doing so. (You don't get a chance to "walk the course" before a trail ride!)

The most fundamental tenet of jumping—look ahead—applies especially strongly when you're out jumping something your horse has never seen. All ring faults—pitching forward, dropping your reins, or cantering on the forehand—will harm you on the trail as well. You need to be a confident and strong jumper on a capable horse before you jump anything on the trail. Don't try anything too new for your horse, like trying to get him over a real wall, complete with crumbling top and rock scattered around. It's much more difficult than having him surmount an oxer of the same height in the ring. School him first over jumps that will fall down if he knocks them, and then advance to their inspirations.

Sometimes you may want your horse to jump a log that has

some grass or other foliage obstructing the top. He may believe that the whole thing is the height of the grass, and refuse. (These types of jumps are called bullfinches in the three-day-eventing world.) The only remedy for this is practice, and since you're not in a show situation, allow your horse to check it out to his satisfaction before backing up and trying to jump it.

Jumping from a light field into a darkened woodsy area is difficult for a horse, so you will need to ride firmly. Coming back, your horse will more likely be happy to oblige and jump into the light.

## Fields

If you're up for a nice canter, few things are more inviting than a wide open and grassy field. But there are a few safety issues to keep in mind. For one, don't set off at a canter or gallop across a field you're not familiar with when the grass is tall. There's no way to know what is hiding in the tall grass, from a car to other animals. If you're cantering across a more easily seen field, still keep an eye on where you are going. A groundhog hole can trip a horse terribly.

If you do want to canter, make sure everyone is ready to go before you take off. And of course, give a "ware hole" if you see one while you are cantering along. Remember, one hole means there are probably more nearby.

## Wildlife

One of the great benefits of trail riding is getting to know the wildlife in your area. You're an animal person to some degree or you would not be a rider, so seeing deer or other animals commonly found in your riding areas is a pleasure. It's important to have some notion of who's around your trails before you head out so that you do not inadvertently harm their habitats.

At the first sound of a human voice, some animals will run, fearing they are near predators. This can destroy animal families if a provider runs away, or inexperienced young animals head out before they can defend themselves.

With predatory animals, like mountain lions or bears, your biggest danger is probably your horse taking off at full gallop, for his innate sense of who is predator and who is prey is intact. Even carnivorous animals like these are unlikely to attack a mounted horse. Still, get away as quickly and quietly as possible, particularly if you think the predator is guarding any young, which may make her very aggressive. If you think you are in a bear's neighborhood, sing, talk, or otherwise make noise as you move along to warn the bear of your presence.

Many predators will see horses as prey animals, even when they have riders. To a predatory animal, horses' footfalls sound like those of a prey animal. This makes them less threatening, which allows wild animals to experience less stress than they would if they heard a person approaching. Let the animals move on while you keep your horse still, then move on yourself.

## Bees and Wasps

Bees, wasps, yellow jackets, and other stinging insects can ruin a trail ride in a hurry. Romeo tripped on a nest of wasps once, and I am still not sure how I stayed on through the bucking and galloping that ensued. I escaped with one sting, but he was stung all over. We weren't very far from the barn, but by the time we got back, his neck and body were dotted with swollen hives from the stings, and I ended up calling the vet to come give him some intravenous antihistamine to remedy the situation. It took a while for him to feel better, and it took me even longer to get him to walk by the spot on the trail where it had happened.

Usually, bees and wasps will not bother you unless your horse, as Romeo did, trips over or steps on a nest. Nests are likely to be found in hollow logs, on the ground under a little ledge, or in a hole in the ground. Some nests are built in trees and a horse could dislodge one by walking underneath. If you think your horse has trod on a nest, start riding as fast and far as you can. If you're in a group, holler a warning and take off. It goes against all

My horse Romeo's neck after a wasp attack. It took a few days for the swellings to go down. (McGraw photo)

the rules of group trail riding, but having a number of horses stung by pursuing bees is guaranteed mayhem, while at least if you orchestrate the getaway you have a chance at escape.

Horses are not allergic to bee stings in the way that some people are. They may get swollen and sore, but most horses will not have the life-threatening anaphylactic reaction some people experience. If you have a known bee sting allergy, carry your epinephrine on your person while you ride. If you get thrown during a bee attack, you want your medicine to be with you, not in your pommel bag or on your fast-escaping horse.

## Orienteering

Orienteering is the art of using a compass to find your way around. It is a good idea to have the basics down when it comes to reading a compass, because if you trail ride on unmarked paths or even get lost on marked ones, knowing where you are on the compass in comparison to where you started from can save you some time, fear, and frustration.

A simple fixed-dial compass will be fine. Stay away from toy compasses, but the bottom of the line, inexpensive kind—even the kind that attaches to a keychain or jacket zipper—is fine. Look at the compass before you head out for your ride, and consult it frequently so that you know where you are going on the compass—north, south, east, or west. This will help you if you lose your way and want to go back the way you came.

These days, many people believe that Global Positioning Systems (GPS) have made the compass obsolete. Because GPS systems, even the battery-powered hand-held ones, take time and effort to learn, they are not always the ideal locating tool for trail riding. For hikers, boaters, and people who love gadgets, the GPS has brought a whole new world of orienteering to outdoor sports and activities. You may find a GPS very helpful, too.

A GPS fits in your hand and is usually about the size of a medium-sized cell phone. It uses satellite technology to tell you exactly where in the world you are. GPS satellites orbit Earth equipped with a clock that helps it know when to broadcast signals to users. The degree of accuracy can be to within as little as a yard.

If you do a lot of riding off marked paths, a GPS can help you plan your ride, and also help figure out where a trail goes once you're out. GPS can work to help you to locate water, and to retrace your steps if you have dropped something. Also, a GPS can keep track of where you went if you want to return to ride the same trail one day. The drawback is that you need to be in a fairly open space for your GPS to work, so if you're lost in a canyon or a very thick forest, you may not get a signal.

## Night Riding

There's a certain romance to riding at night. The moonlight is beautiful, and everything just seems so special when you're taking such a big turn from the mundane. Horses see well at night. Your horse regularly grazes all night long without running into the fence. And if you give it a minute, you will probably be surprised and impressed by your own night vision, as well. Some people like to ride without any additional lights to preserve this natural feeling. If you do want to ride with some light, though, try a lightstick attached to a bridle or saddle instead of a flashlight (white light is what destroys night vision for both you and your horse.) Take a flashlight, though, for use in an emergency. You don't want to be crouched trying to fasten an Easyboot by the albeit pleasant glow of a lightstick.

No artificial light is the best way to preserve your night vision and your horse's. But if trail riding without some white light makes you anxious, you can use a headlamp, and be forewarned that your vision outside the beam will not be acute. Also, get your horse used to it before heading out, because many horses will spook when a bright light is suddenly turned on during a time they are used to being in the dark.

Reflective gear is a must at dark or even at dusk, especially if you will be anywhere near a road. Reflective bands—or even ones with battery-powered flashing lights—can go around your ankles, your horse's ankles, and your helmet. You can also wear a reflective vest over your riding clothes. Give yourself every possible advantage when riding at night. Car drivers will not be looking for you.

## Hunting

Hunting and horseback riding have a somewhat odd relationship. The two sports merge famously in foxhunting, and some game hunters use horses to pack the animals they have shot. Whatever your politics on the subject of hunting game, horse people and hunters do share much open space. If you ride in an area where hunting is permitted, you need to take precautions to ensure that no firearm-related emergencies arise.

Riding on non-posted land during hunting season is dangerous because hunters, especially inexperienced or alcoholically impaired ones, can mistake a horse for a deer or elk. Always wear blaze orange when you are riding near a hunting area to be safe. Vests, helmet covers, and saddle pads all come in this color. You can also tie a blaze orange kerchief to your horse's tail and wear one around your neck.

If you're simply out on a posted trail and happen to pass some hunters, be prepared for your horse to become unsettled. Some hunters train pack horses to help carry their game out of the woods, and horses unused to this sight may spook at the smell of fresh kill. Animal blood can scare horses, and hunters have plenty on and around them. Even the sight of a pack heaped on top of another horse, combined with the meat's odor, may rattle your horse. In fact, some trail class designers use animal hides as obstacles because so many horses need to be trained to pass them calmly.

## Poison Ivy and Other Poisonous Plants

Poison ivy, oak, and sumac, the banes of people, don't bother horses. They can eat them and rub up against them with no ill effects. So there is no reason to worry about your horse if he gets too near any of these plants.

The problem is that people are allergic to urushiol, the oil that the plants contain. Since the oil is what causes the irritation, a horse can easily transmit the oil through contact if, for example, he touches poison ivy and then you touch him. Poison ivy grows on vines as well as in shrubs on the ground, so a trail horse can swipe by some without anyone noticing. If he steps through some ground-covering poison ivy, he will carry the rash-causing oil on his hooves. The oil does not really wear off. It is very potent and can be carried on tack, boots, and other equipment for a year or so. If you think any of your clothing or tack has been contaminated, clean it well before using it again. Also, if you think you have come into contact with poison ivy on the trail, don't go to the bathroom or wipe your face until you have washed up thoroughly, because you can spread the oil all over yourself without even knowing it.

Always carry a product that removes urushiol like Tecnu® or Ivarest® with you in your saddle pad or saddlebag if you know you are allergic to any of these plants. You can be trail riding, and your horse will brush against one of them, transferring the oil onto you, and if you are miles from home without a place to wash it off, you're a candidate for the miserable rash that ensues, since if it stays on you for more than about twenty minutes, it bonds with your skin and will not wash off. Because poison ivy does not

"Leaves of three, let it be," is one way to remember what poison ivy looks like. (McGraw photo)

affect horses, it's hard to know if your horse has gotten into any out in the pasture or on the trail. Then when you're grooming him or giving him a pat, the oil can get onto you and eventually give you the rash. If you suspect this may have happened, wash up as soon as you get back to the barn. Remember, urushiol gets smeared on one thing, and can contaminate another and another until it is washed from everything it has come in contact with.

## Ticks

Ticks are more than an annoyance. We now know that they can transmit serious infections like Lyme disease to people and horses. Ticks can also give horses *Ehrlichia* organisms that can result in blood cell damaging illnesses. Pyrethin-containing fly sprays and repellents guard against ticks. But while you may just allow a mist to settle on your horse in order to repel flies, you need to let it soak in to ward off ticks. If ticks are a problem in your area, every couple of weeks or so, apply a soaking amount of pyrethin or permethrins at least to his legs. An old-school solution is to apply petroleum jelly or a mentholated rub around his ankles to prevent the ticks from traveling upward.

If you want to take a tick out, don't use rubbing alcohol. This folk remedy will, unfortunately, just leave you with a fragrant tick. Use tweezers, and pull, grabbing hold where the tick's head is attached to the skin. Don't worry about leaving the mouth attached; that's another myth. If some tick is left behind, it won't hurt your horse. Some people swear by drops of milk of magnesia as an ointment for a tick bite.

Lyme disease is more common in pasture-kept and trail horses for the obvious reason that they are outside more often than their stall-kept counterparts. It is still, however, a relatively rare disease, but if you hear of cases in your area, and your horse has some of the following symptoms, suspect Lyme. In the early stages, horses have a mild fever and sometimes swollen legs, which in horses, can be anything, so Lyme is rarely diagnosed at this point. It's when a horse's joints and muscles seem chronically in pain that a veterinarian may suspect Lyme disease. Some people might even think their horse has EPM (the neurological disease equine protozoal myelitis) because of a Lyme horse's shuffling or trouble walking. Veterinarians rely on a combination of factors to decide that a horse probably has Lyme disease: a series of blood tests, the odd lameness that many Lyme disease sufferers have, and living in an area known to have deer ticks. (The blood tests indicate exposure to Lyme disease, but not necessarily infection from it.) The good news about Lyme disease is that it does respond to antibiotics, and many horses make a recovery.

## Environmentally Friendly Trail Riding

Compared to anything with a motor, horses are low-impact on the environment. But because of their weight and the amount of stress they place on any trail, they have more of an impact than hikers. Whether or not you think of yourself as an environmentalist, the fact that you enjoy trail riding means that the outdoors is important to you. So preserving the environment should be as well, since it means more trail riding. Also, many parks that offer bridle paths also exhort you to minimize the impact you and your horse have on the natural resources of the parks. Phrases like

"Leave no trace," "Leave only footprints and take only memories," and "Pack it in, pack it out," are common postings and make sense to trail riders who want to keep their trails rideable and with a future. Much of it is in your attitude—do the best you can. Of course your horse is going to tread on vegetation, and of course his heavy hooves will contribute somewhat to erosion. Many environmentalists believe that horses should not be allowed on trails at all because they're so hard on them. But as riders, we have an obligation to make an effort to cause as little harm as possible.

It may mean giving up something you wanted to do, such as cutting across a forest or stopping to tie your horse to a tree. We as trail riders should listen to what our strictest equestrian colleagues have to say, because as the saying goes, "They're not making any more land," and we need beautiful spaces to enjoy trail riding.

Serious environmentalists will tell you not to tie a horse at all, for good reason—horses chew trees, they ruin the soil beneath their feet, etc. But I think there is a middle ground here, and ways to do little damage while still enjoying your sport. There are good books on this topic, and organizations such as NOLS (the National Outdoor Leadership School) that work to minimize impact on the environment. For horse campers, learning to use a picket or high line is worthwhile. For the rest of us, a store-bought tree saver will do most of the work for you.

Walking instead of trotting and cantering is good for the trail. The wetter the soil, the worse it is to ride at speed on it. So save your faster riding for dry, packed trails. The more trail gets displaced, the more erosion takes place, which is what we're trying to prevent. Hobbling helps keep a horse from churning up soil when he is tied.

When riding on trails, minimize your impact on them by riding in single file. As much fun as it is to ride next to a buddy, it's bad for the trails because it widens them. When you come across a muddy section, urge your horse to go through rather than around it. If you make a wide path around the mud, you will effectively clear a new path, which is not good for the trail system and the surrounding areas. People will then start following your

Riding single file
helps to preserve
the trail.

new trail, which will just get muddy itself. Cleaning your horse up after a trail ride is just part of the day; ride through mud. This is especially key during a spring thaw, when everything gets so wet. Stick to the trails.

Same goes for snow. If some snow covers the path, ride through it instead of trying to circumvent it. If you can't see the trail, just go as close as possible to where you think it might be. Otherwise, the snow will eventually melt and an entire new trail will be hacked through where there was less snow.

When you stop for a break, or to let everyone catch up, choose your spot carefully. Stamping horses can really wreak havoc on the ground and ground cover. Find somewhere less vulnerable to damage, like rock or sand if possible.

When you encounter hikers on the trail and each of you are on either side of a barrier (like a fallen tree), it's best if they step off the trail and hold still while you get over the tree, usually by stepping over it, although if you have to jump, you have to jump. Walking around obstacles hurts the terrain, and hikers weigh less than horse and rider teams. Your goal is not to create an alternative trail. Your next responsibility is to alert whoever is in charge of the trail—a park ranger or a planning board. They should have the obstacle removed so others don't keep having this problem and the trail stays whole.

Try not to let your horse leave urine or manure in a stream, because it's bad for the fish and any other animals who drink that water. Because it takes horses so long to settle into a urinating position, it's usually pretty easy to ask them to move along if they are in a stream. (Most horses won't want to urinate in water anyway—too much splashing.) With manure, just do the best you can to keep it out of the water.

Here are some "commandments" written by leading conservationists to keep in mind as you ride:

From the "Back Country Horsemen" [1]

a. The horseman shall not keep horses longer than it takes to unpack or pack them in any campsite normally used by hikers [or other trail users]. (We suggest horsemen stay away from such sites if possible.)

b. The horseman shall not tie his stock, for more than a short period of time [minimal time], directly to a tree.

c. The horseman shall not cut switchbacks.

d. The horseman shall not leave a campfire unattended.

e. The horseman shall properly dispose of all manure, bailing twine, wire and waste hay in camp areas, trailheads, or loading areas.

f. The horseman shall abide by administrative rules and regulations affecting the area he/she is in.

[1] *Back Country Horsemen of America Guidebook* published by Hungry Horse News, Columbia Falls, Montana. This publication was prepared by the Back Country Horsemen of America and published in partnership with the Northern, Intermountain, Pacific Northwest, Rocky Mountain and Pacific Southwest Regions USDA Forest Service.

g. The horseman shall recognize the fragility of the back-country environment and practice minimum-impact techniques at all times.

h. Be considerate of other visitors (users of the landscape).

An American nonprofit organization called Leave No Trace has established rules for minimizing impact on the wilderness. Their rules for horse use are:[2]

1. Plan ahead and prepare.

2. Travel and camp on durable surfaces.

3. Dispose of waste properly.

4. Leave what you find.

5. Minimize campfire impact.

6. Respect wildlife.

7. Be considerate of other visitors.

Although these rules are primarily intended for serious back-country horsepeople, most apply to us as everyday trail riders as well. Look into these organizations and publications if you are interested in horse packing and backcountry riding. By maintaining a good reputation as stewards of the outdoors, trail riders keep viable more places to ride.

The Backcountry Horsemen's advice to avoid cutting switchbacks, or new trails, applies even if you are riding on the most well-groomed trail in a state park. Your planning ahead and preparation can help the wilderness because—to take just one example—you won't need to build a campfire when you bring food that does not need heating. For riders, good planning can be the difference between hacking through miles of underbrush and possibly damaging plant life and getting lost, or having the appropriate maps and gear for the trails you want to ride.

[2] *Leave No Trace Outdoor Skills and Ethics: Back Country Horse Use*. National Outdoor Leadership School. LNT Skills and Ethics Series. Vol. 3.2.

Riders should always pack out whatever they pack in. Especially since our horses carry so much of the things we are packing in in the first place, we have no excuse not to bring it back out with us. This includes lunch trash, toilet paper, water bottles, and chewing gum. Mountain bikers no doubt wish we would pack the horse manure out with us, but there is a limit. Riders can, however, keep a muck bucket in their trailers and clean up the parking area or trailhead before they go home, then dispose of the manure however they usually do at the barn. Leaving what you find is especially good for the environment. This applies to flowers, rocks, plants, and animals. Don't try to lure that cute bunny rabbit home with you, or pick flowers while you're trail riding. These plants and animals are supposed to stay at home in the woods, and removing them makes the wilderness ecosystem vulnerable. And don't feed animals you see out on the trail, because it disrupts their natural diet and can make them a nuisance to future trail users.

# 7 | Handling
## Emergencies

**E**very horse sport has inherent dangers, making it likely that situations can arise and threaten the health or general well-being of a horse or a rider. The easiest way to handle emergencies is to avoid them, but things can go wrong regardless of the best preparation. Even so, you can take precautions that will lessen the likelihood of their happening.

Trail riding often means that, necessarily, you will be far from the kind of help you may be able to get from a suburban boarding facility or in a city riding ring. Trail riders may not consider themselves outdoor enthusiasts in the same way back-packers and wildlife photographers are. Safety measures that any serious hiker would take are often ignored by trail riders, who tend to think of the "rider" before the "trail." As time-consuming as careful planning can be, it will pay off. From the moment you set out on a trail ride to the moment you return to the barn, precautions will make your ride more enjoyable and more safe.

# Riding Alone

Trail riding alone is never the safest way to go. Too many things can happen when you are by yourself in the woods with only your horse for help. Yet riding alone is common for a number of reasons. It is hard to coordinate schedules with other people, and when you want to turn back from a trail ride when no one else does this may mean you are riding solo. And there are times you would like to be alone with your horse. There is something very peaceful about riding along a trail with only the sound of your horse's breathing and his hooves.

So when you ride alone, take even more safeguards than you ordinarily would. Make sure your cell phone has a charged battery, and that your tack and your horses' shoes are in good shape. Don't push any part of your ride; a day you're on your own is not the best day to check out a new trail, or ride by something your horse has never seen. Stick to your more familiar paths, and

Sometimes you just want to ride alone. That's fine, as long as you exercise care.

keep things simple. Then you can concentrate on enjoying your time with your horse, and save the challenges for a day when you have a buddy.

Often, the only way people know who is at the barn and who has left is by checking the barn parking lot. If you and your horse don't return by the end of the day, but your car is sitting in the lot, someone will notice that something is wrong. (If your horse lives in a stall, his absence would be noticed at feeding time, but if your horse lives in a large herd, his absence may not be as obvious.) This is a last resort method; someone should know where you are before the barn manager realizes your car is still there, and you're out on the trail with a broken leg or worse.

A bulletin board can be used to let people at the barn know where you are heading and when you expect to return. (McGraw photo)

Boarding facilities with large trail rider populations may have a ride board, usually a chalkboard or dry-erase board where you write down where you are going, what horse you are riding, and the time you leave. "2:00 Sunday. Jen and Scarlett are riding the upper loop—stopping to eat lunch at the Falls." As soon as you return, you erase your note from the board.

**Everyday Trail Riding**

This way, if anything happens, someone back at the barn will know to go looking for you, and where to begin the search. It's not entirely foolproof, because you may change your mind as you ride along, or get held up by a sudden thunderstorm, or double back earlier than expected. But it still gives an idea of your whereabouts so that someone knows where you are when you don't return.

If the barn does not have a ride board, then be sure to call your spouse or a friend before you head out and say where you intend to ride as well as when you think you will be back. He or she can wait for your call, and then contact someone at the barn— or come looking for you—if you don't return by the time you said.

## The Buddy System

The buddy system simply means that you do not ride alone, and that you are responsible for one other rider's well-being, and she yours. So if she needs to dismount for any reason, and the rest of the group goes on ahead, you stay behind. If she is struggling to close a gate, you dismount and help hold her horse. Even if you need to turn back, your buddy leaves with you to make sure you get back to the barn safely.

## Cell Phones

Cellular, or mobile, phones have been a boon to riders. Show riders use them to keep in touch with trainers and family on the show grounds, and everyone agrees that they have made life more convenient. They can be a huge help to the trail rider, as well. A cell phone can mean the difference between being able to stay with a hurt friend and having to ride off for help. It can mean that if you're alone and something happens, you can call the barn and have someone come fetch you. Should you be lost, you may be able to talk to someone who can help you find your way again.

That said, though, many of the best trail rides are out of cell phone reach. Also, batteries lose their charge, and anything mechanical can break. If you're not conscientious about recharging your phone (and many of us are not), you won't be able to use it. If your horse is particularly frolicsome during a creek crossing, your phone may fall and be ruined. So it's best not to depend solely on your phone. A phone does not mean that riding alone is safe, although it does give you a measure of security if you ride in an area with service.

Your phone can be carried in several ways. There are cell phone holders that clip onto the dee rings on an English saddle, or go over the horn on a Western one. The problem with these holders is that if you and your horse are separated—if he throws you, or if he somehow slips his hobbles and takes off—he has the phone. They can smack the horse as you ride along, especially at the trot, and some horses don't like them. If you are comfortable wearing a fanny pack when you ride, then it can hold your phone. Vertically hanging phone holsters can bang on the saddle, so one that stows the phone horizontally is best.

Keep the phone on your body if you can. There are ankle and arm holders for phones, and many smaller ones just slip right into a pocket, which is handy when it is cool enough to wear a jacket. Cell phones in jeans pockets tend to fall out while you are trotting, and the next thing you know your trail ride has turned into a phone search. Making your buddies call your phone on their cell phones while you listen for the ring is a sure way to ruin a trail ride. If you carry your phone on a belt hook, make sure it stays on your side, not near the center of your back, where it could cause injury to your spine if you fell on it.

Put your barn number and the number of the park police or rangers in your phone's memory, so you're not struggling to recall a number or search for a scrap of paper when you need it. Your phone should always be on silent when you're on horseback. A loud ringing that sounds like a chorus from *Carmen* can scare your horse, particularly when it seems to be coming from you. Also, you don't need to take any call that will take your attention away from riding—it requires enough concentration as it is.

# Missing

If a rider heads out for a trail ride and her horse returns, or neither is seen for hours longer than their ride should have taken, it's time to get concerned and contact local authorities. When someone is reported missing, the first thing you need to do is figure out how long the person has been missing, and how urgent the situation is. Is this person an experienced rider? Does she have any medical problems that could mean that the situation is life-threatening? Think of anything you can that might help people search.

The people who assemble to search for a person who has not been missing too long are called a "hasty team" in search-and-rescue circles. The riding version of the hasty team is usually the people who are at the barn or the trailer parking lot when the person is discovered missing. They mount up and try to go the same way the missing rider has gone. The sooner the search commences, the better for the rider.

Lost people (and their horses) tend to travel in circles if they are lost in a flat area. If the terrain is hilly, they are probably heading downhill over a unobstructed path.

Muster a hasty team to search for a missing rider.

For a search to be efficient and successful, ask yourself what parts of the trail are the most complicated. Are there places it is easy to get turned around? How familiar is the person's horse with the area? Chances are, an old school horse who knows the trails well will get a beginner home, but a new horse will have to depend on luck to get home.

There is some truth to this old saw that horses can all find their way home. If they are lost near their usual pasture or barn, most horses will make it back eventually. But well-mannered horses will listen to their riders, no matter if she is turning him away from the barn. After all, that's what she does every time they set out. Also, a horse who is in a new place, although he has a better chance than his rider of getting back to their starting point, can easily become disoriented. He's not going to remember where the trailer was parked every time, and he may take a rider off through an impassable forest instead of sticking to trails.

## If You're Lost

Always keep track of where you are riding, even if you're not in control of a group. Watch trail markers, observe landmarks, and think about where you are heading. That way, if someone needs to guide help to the group, or you need or want to return to the trailers for any reason, you will know where you are. No matter how reliable your leader or riding buddy is, you should depend on yourself first.

If you're the one lost, your biggest (and hardest) job is to stay calm. If you get panicky, not only will you lose your own chance to think clearly, but your horse may get panicky as well. Then you're stuck having to handle a fearful horse as well as finding your way back. So take deep breaths and assess the situation, and stay calm as you look for familiar landmarks. If you are riding with someone else, don't let her get panicked either. You need each other's help, and if both of you lose your heads, you also lose your chances of getting out sooner rather than later.

Stand still and listen for traffic, or children playing, or any other sound that indicates that you might be near people. Stay

quiet and listen for a few minutes, while your ears adjust to the sounds around you.

Screaming for help is a bad idea, and not just because it will scare the horses. It will make your throat sore, eventually cause you to lose your voice, and often is not even heard. If you do a lot of backcountry riding, it's a good idea to carry a whistle and get your horse acclimated to the shrill sound. If you do a lot of riding at night, another helpful signaling tool is a little strobe light, which makes you very visible. If it's day, even a little mirror (packed for this purpose) can work. Try this trick: hold the mirror up and use it to reflect sunlight.

Fires are very visible. Building a fire is risky around horses, but if the situation gets dire, you may need to do it. Use wet materials (leaves, branches) to make your fire last. If you think things have gotten to the point where people may be searching for you by air, you can make strip signals on a hillside or field out of any kind of wood. Try to find the straightest pieces possible so they don't look like random piles of wood. Your reins or other

If you are lost, you can hear better—and possibly figure out where you are sooner—if you stand still for a minute.

bits of gear can work as well. The international language of strip signals is a Y for yes, I need help. An N means no, I don't need help. An arrow points which way you are going, and a cross means you need medical help.

If it looks like you are going to be stuck outside overnight, you need to find some shelter and a way to secure your horse. Shelter will keep you from having to use valuable body heat to stay warm. A low-lying evergreen tree can be a huge help if you're looking for protection. The forest floor should be padded and there should not be too much room overhead, so that you can warm the space. Although tying your horse to a tree is frowned upon because it's bad for the tree, if you don't have hobbles with you and are in an emergency situation, you may have to do it. As for you, use your wits. Even a pile of leaves under a tree is better than no shelter at all. Try to avoid any weak-looking tree limbs, because they may break off and hurt you.

If you can find water, that's a big help. If you ride in the backcountry often, consider carrying water purification tablets with you. Otherwise, it's best to avoid indeterminate water unless you and your horse are very thirsty. Energy bars are another good idea for a backcountry pack.

To avoid getting lost in the first place, carry a map or GPS. If you're riding in a park, make sure you stick to the trail you started off on—the trail symbols should stay the same, so that you're following a blue square the whole way even if you cross a trail marked with an orange triangle for portions of it. Every so often, look behind you, so that landmarks imprint in your memory in both directions. Notice how many turns you've made. If you are struggling to find your way back, you may want to leave markers for yourself, such as tape, but this isn't a good habit to get into since it does make the woods look trashy.

# Medical Emergencies

Medical emergencies can and will happen on the trail. Be sure your horse is in good health before you set out. Here is what is normal for a horse:

Temperature: 99–100 degrees Fahrenheit

Heart Rate: 28–44 beats per minute

Mucous membranes and gums: salmon-colored

Nasal discharge: clear is ok, opaque or yellow is not

Knowing your horse as you do makes you his best diagnostician. If your horse tends not to get overheated, but returns drenched in sweat on a coolish day, you may suspect something is wrong, although the sweat itself is not abnormal. Something may just seem "off" about him. If you feel strongly enough about it, call the vet. It's better to irritate your veterinarian than to have something happen to your horse that you could have prevented.

Trust yourself if you think something may be wrong with your horse. You know him best.

(And if your vet really seems that annoyed when you are truly concerned, you may need a new vet.)

Medical emergencies serve as a reminder not to ask your horse to do more than he is fit to do. A horse who is pulled out of the pasture after a month's vacation and asked to go on a long, hilly trail ride on a hot day is at risk for dehydration as well as sprains and other stress-related injuries.

The best way to tell that something is wrong with your horse is simply to know him well. Never underestimate your "feelings" when it comes to your horse. You, more than even a veterinarian sometimes, know when something is just not right. If something about your horse makes you uneasy, ask your veterinarian to pay a call. You may be wrong, but the worst thing that will happen is that you will have to pay a fee for a barn call and the horse will be fine. If you're right, your instinct could save your horse some pain or speed the treatment of an illness.

Once you're out on a trail, your horse may exhibit some conditions that give you concern. A drooling horse (who has not been in the clover) may have something stuck in his throat. It can also mean rabies, which is rare in horses, but possible. And anything wrong with a horse's eyes should be attended to immediately, because an infection can lead to serious vision problems or even blindness. In that case, you need to get your horse home and into a darkened area until the vet can get there.

If your horse is fairly balanced, but seems to be going heavily on his forehand, you know something is wrong. Obvious stumbling or tripping down hills can indicate weakness or increasing lameness. If your horse is constantly refusing to move forward, he might be in pain (or just balky—this is one of those things you have to judge yourself). If he won't take one of his leads, that side may be sore anywhere from the foot to the shoulder.

While you are standing still, your horse may not be totally immobile, but he should be at ease and calm. If he is shifting constantly or "tapping" one foot, he might be trying to tell you something about which foot, leg, or shoulder is troubling him. A horse who paws and paws may be wanting to roll, which could indicate a problem in his gut. Emotional or psychological shifts can indicate trouble, too. Is your normally engaged horse not even looking around as he walks? Do his eyes look glassy? He could be feeling ill.

To guard against your horse picking up any infectious disease when you're trail riding, don't let your horse touch noses with other horses you meet. Don't use the troughs that some parks set out, but bring your own buckets to fill, and let your horse drink from them. And avoid sharing them.

We need to be prepared for human emergencies as well. If you have any kind of special medical condition, like diabetes or epilepsy, make sure you are wearing your alert bracelet or dog tag as you ride. People allergic to bee stings should carry epinephrine with them at all times, too; a horse can easily tread on a nest and leave you with a serious sting, far from the nearest emergency room. Keep your medication with you and learn to use it.

# Rabies

Rabies is rare in horses, but it is also fatal. Your veterinarian should have your horse on a rabies vaccine schedule, but even the vaccine isn't entirely effective. Most inoculated horses who have been bitten by a rabid animal do recover, though, especially when given a booster shot after a bite. Because they encounter many different animals as they work, trail horses are particularly susceptible to rabies.

If you see a wild animal, like a skunk or raccoon, acting oddly as you ride, stay away. Bats and coyotes can also be carriers. Seeing any of these nocturnal creatures wandering around slowly or in an unprotected area during the day should give you cause for concern. If the animal does not startle when it sees you, that's further cause for concern.

A horse with a leg bite will take longer to show signs of rabies than a horse whose face gets bitten. An infected horse can seem very depressed and then seem a little spacey. He can also seem "rabid"—uncharacteristically furious and aggressive. Next, neurological symptoms—like pronounced stumbling and falling—present themselves until he can no longer get himself up off the ground. The horse will usually die within a week. If there is a case of rabies in your area, news usually travels fast from barn to barn. But it still pays to check with local authorities each year. If you see a dead animal on your property or on a trail, have your animal control officer test the body for rabies.

## West Nile Virus

West Nile Virus (WNV) has received a lot of attention in recent years because of its deleterious effects on people as well as horses. WNV, like rabies, may be more common in trail horses because of the prolonged exposure they have while under saddle as well as at home. WNV is spread by mosquitoes.

You can suspect WNV if you live in an area where WNV has been diagnosed, and your horse has been around a lot of mosquito-ridden areas, such as standing water or ponds, or has been out at dusk, when mosquitoes are the most active. Symptoms to watch for include a lack of coordination in the hindquarters and hind legs. The horse's lower lip droops, and the rest of his body is uncoordinated as well, with some horses even falling down. Drooling, staggering, and other neurological signs of trouble are all common with WNV. Horses can recover from WNV, but they need veterinary attention. Because the symptoms are often so dramatic, you will probably call the vet if your horse appears this unusual, and be sure to mention that you suspect a lot of exposure to mosquitoes. Your vet will probably know if there have been any local cases, and how many.

## Equine Infectious Anemia

Whenever you ride at a new park or on a new path, you will be asked for proof of a Coggins test. This is proof of a negative equine infectious anemia test. Equine infectious anemia (EIA) used to be called swamp fever, and it poses a danger to show and trail horses because they travel so widely. This is why you're always asked to carry that proof of negative test results with you.

EIA is transmitted by horseflies or other insects (in rare

cases, an infected hypodermic needle) who get the blood from the infected horse into a new horse. Symptoms take weeks to develop, and include a sporadic high fever, fatigue and loss of energy, swollen belly and legs, and anemia. Unfortunately, because the virus keeps changing, it is not curable. The horse seems healthy again, but the virus is inside him, mutating and finding new ways to survive. Sadly, horses who test positive for EIA usually have to be put down, kept on permanent quarantine, or donated to a research facility. Keep your Coggins test current, and don't ride with people who don't do so.

## Salmonella

We know what salmonella poisoning is because of its link to raw eggs, and restaurant menus may contain warnings about some foods that are traditionally prepared with raw eggs. But salmonella can hurt your trail horse, too. In fact, because salmonella is often transmitted by horses eating off the ground in affected areas, trail horses are one of the most at-risk equine groups.

Salmonella is everywhere; many horses have some strain of the bacteria already. But when a very potent strain, or a large amount of bacteria, affects one area, all the horses are at risk. It is spread by horses grazing where salmonella-infected manure has been deposited. The droppings can have been from another horse, but they can also be from other animals. If a carrier leaves droppings on a trail, and your horse stops to graze nearby, he could get infected.

If you hear of a local outbreak, keep your horse at home for a while. If he has been on antibiotics, or any kind of immunity-lowering prescription drug, he may be more likely to contract salmonella than other horses.

Salmonella poisoning can result in a horse having serious watery diarrhea, a fever, and even founder, or laminitis. Antibiotics are not too successful in treating salmonella, so a horse often only needs time, rest, and care to recover. His manure will have the bacteria for a while, too, so it will be best to keep him fairly confined until your veterinarian decides he is all right.

# Colic

Colic is another word for a horse's stomach cramps and discomfort. Colic can be a result of impaction of food, gas, or, more seriously, a twisted intestine. Serious colic can result in real illness or even death. Trail horses are at risk when they have recently started eating something different, like grain or spring grass. Horses who are under duress are prone to colic, so if your horse was in the trailer for the first time, or does not like leaving home, he could be more inclined to colic. Lack of water can lead to colic, which is just one of the reasons to keep encouraging your horse to drink out on the trail.

Suspect colic out on the trail if your horse keeps pawing or trying to lie down. He may also hike up a leg and seem to be kicking at his own stomach. If he is drenched in sweat while other horses who have done the same work seem comfortable, or if he keeps curling his upper lip over and over again, these are indications of colic as well.

If you think your horse is colicking, check his capillary refill

Dismount from a horse you believe to be colicking, and slowly walk him home.

time by pressing on his gums. Check to see if they have turned dark. Listen to his belly, too, because absence of gut sounds can mean colic. If you have a well-stocked first aid kit, give the horse some Banamine®, just as you would at the barn. Do not give him acepromazine, though, because it can make his blood pressure drop. Your main job is to get him home by leading him slowly, and have the veterinarian see him as soon as possible.

## Tying Up, or Azoturia, or Monday Morning Disease

Muscle degeneration that causes serious cramping and agony goes by several names: tying up, azoturia, and Monday morning disease. No one knows exactly what causes this condition, but it is most common in horses who are suddenly worked hard after resting (hence, Monday morning disease). If your horse stops and won't go on, and appears in obvious pain, particularly around his hindquarters (he may be stamping haltingly, or swishing his tail around), he may be tying up. This is the only thing you should not try to "walk him out" of. Instead, keep offering him water, and if you have it in your trail bag, give him some bute. Otherwise, call for help and medicine before trying to get him home.

Besides keeping your horse in regular work so that he is used to being ridden and exerting himself, you can also prevent tying up by keeping his diet steady. Rich alfalfa or grain seems to push some horses toward tying up as well. A rarer cause of tying up is a selenium deficiency, which is something you would be aware of, because if selenium is rare in your area, most horse people you know probably supplement with it. If you are not sure, ask.

## Bleeding

Horses get cut on the trail. Jutting sticks and sharp ledges make for potential hazards, and on urban trails a glass cut is not out of the question. Horses can lose about a gallon of blood without too many ill effects, so sometimes what looks like way too much blood to a person may not be as bad as it seems. But getting a wound to stop bleeding is the first priority when a horse is cut. The bleeding needs to stop before the cut can get better.

Bandages—gauze and some Vetrap™ or other tight bandaging material—are best. But if you don't have these things, you can use a handkerchief or even your t-shirt or bare hands to staunch the bleeding. The longer you wait to get a veterinarian to look at the cut, the greater the risk of infection. So head for home right away when something serious happens. If the wound has flayed the skin layer and you can see muscle or other underlying tissue, it's going to need stitches (and your horse will need a tetanus shot). Bandage snugly, but don't leave a really tight bandage on for more than a couple of hours.

## Lost Shoe

Losing a shoe is not a life-threatening emergency; nevertheless a horse who is used to being shod can get hurt quickly without a shoe. A couple of sore steps may make a horse unwilling to bear weight, and being left miles from home with a lame horse can turn into an emergency situation fast. This is why you should keep your horse on a shoeing schedule and check him carefully for loose nails before you head out on a long trail ride.

The other thing to do is to carry a shoe replacement—a plastic "boot" that fits over the hoof and protects it until a new shoe can be put on, sort of like a "doughnut" spare tire in a car. Some replacements fasten with pressure wires, and others use heavy-duty Velcro. "Easyboot" is the most common brand name and popular product, so you might hear many people call all hoof protectors "easyboots," or "Davis boots," or "medicine boots," although there are many different brands.

Finally, if your horse is not prone to losing shoes but happens to on the trail, look at the foot before you consider remounting. Some horses may be fine carrying you home with a lost shoe; others may not, and you will need to get off and walk home. Check and see what made your horse lose his shoe, and use

A lost shoe can ruin a trail ride and hurt the horse's foot. (McGraw photo)

common sense. Don't ride on a torn or cracked hoof, or if your horse is obviously lame (bobbing his head, favoring the shoeless foot). If the shoe seems to have just fallen off, you may be all right riding the horse at an easy pace until you get back to the barn. But when you get home, if your horse's foot still seems hot or otherwise hurt, call the veterinarian and have your farrier come out to reshoe the horse. Chronic shoe loss is a matter to take up with your farrier too, for it may mean that a change in your horse's shoeing is necessary.

## Heatstroke

Any horse can be prone to heatstroke in the summer. (See Chapter 6 for more on heat.) Heatstroke occurs when your horse can't get rid of excess heat through sweat, the way he normally does. He can lose oxygen because blood is routed differently, and he can collapse or even die.

A horse with heatstroke can have a temperature of over 104 degrees Fahrenheit. He may pant like a dog and even stop sweating. His gums will lose their healthy pink color and get dark red, and he won't get better even when you stop him and let him stand in the shade. Sponge him off with any water you have, and try to get him to drink. Then lead him home slowly, stopping often to let him rest. Call the vet when you get home.

## Hypothermia

When the body's core temperature gets too low, a condition called hypothermia develops. Compared to long-distance swimmers, skiers, and other winter athletes, properly suited trail riders are not at great risk for hypothermia. Nevertheless, if you get lost in a blizzard or on a bitterly cold day, it is possible.

Signs of hypothermia include slow breathing or pulse, mental confusion, and skin that is cold to the touch. Keep someone whom you suspect is hypothermic in a prone position, because this position makes it easier for the heart to get blood to the brain. Try to warm the person with coats and blankets, and send for help as soon as possible. In drastic cases and if it will be a long time until help arrives, another person's body heat can be used to warm up the hypothermic person. Time is really of the essence when dealing with hypothermia, so trying to stabilize the person's core temperature is key.

Theoretically, horses can get hypothermic as well. It is very rare in healthy adult horses, although elderly or arthritic horses who spend a lot of time lying on cold ground in the winter could get hypothermia. After an extended fall in an icy river, for example, a trail horse might develop a low core temperature. He, too, will seem as if he is in shock, and may stumble. A hypothermic horse needs immediate veterinary attention.

## Lameness

A horse can come up lame for any number of reasons. Sometimes the reason doesn't even matter—what does is that you recognize when your horse is going lame so that you can get off him, lead him home, and call the vet.

If your horse suddenly seems lame, dismount and examine his foot. He may have picked up a rock.

The most common way to find out if he's lame is to know him well. You are the most familiar with his gaits and way of going, and if something just seems off to you, it probably is. Your horse will send you some signals to let you know he is in pain as he walks down the trail.

Probably the most obvious is if he stops or "pulls up lame." If your horse is not balky, but is suddenly refusing to go forward even when you ask, he may be in pain. If he is nodding his head as he walks along, he is "head-bobbing lame." His head will go down when his sound foot hits the ground and pop up when the hurt foot does. Any extreme high-headedness can mean that one of his front legs or feet is hurting him. If your horse feels very choppy in his strides or is dragging his feet, that may suggest lameness as well.

If you can get to a hard surface, like packed dirt or pavement, you may be able to hear your horse's lameness. He will use the good hooves in a "louder" way, while he restrains himself and holds back so that a sore foot is used more "softly." While some people have a natural knack for detecting exactly where a lameness is, many need the veterinarian to figure it out through watching and flexion tests. If your horse is showing any of the above symptoms of discomfort, your job is to lead him home slowly and let the vet do the detective work later.

Carrying bute on the trail with you is a good idea. It can alleviate some lameness, because it helps to minimize the inflammation of a wound or sprain. But the same warnings about bute apply on the trail as well—bute can mask symptoms of pain, so be careful with it. If your horse is trying to tell you what hurts, bute can silence that. Ask your veterinarian when bute might be helpful for your horse.

## Foot Wounds

Any horse can get foot wounds, but a trail horse's chances are even greater. What with nails, sharp rocks, and glass, there are many ways for horses to damage their feet on the trail. Although foot wounds can get serious very fast, if they are cleaned and dressed within a day or less, lifelong repercussions like scarring and chronic lameness can be avoided.

Any of the five basic kinds of wounds—abrasions, incised wounds, lacerations, avulsions, and puncture wounds—can occur in the horse's skin as well as in his foot. Abrasions (or scrapes) usually involve the outermost layers of skin. In the foot, they are usually seen in the coronary band, where the tough covering is thinnest. Typically, any injury that truly hurts the foot will be more serious than an abrasion, but in some instances, such as an unshod horse scraping himself on rough asphalt, abrasions can cause great damage to feet. Incised wounds (sharp cuts) are rarer, but can occur if a horse on a littered trail comes into contact with a piece of rough-edged sheet metal or something similarly sharp, and gets an almost surgical-looking cut. The horny nature of hoof probably would keep the wound from gaping open as a skin incision might, but the incision itself is still serious.

Lacerations are cuts with damaged edges, and most of the hoof will usually split rather than tear the way skin would if lacerated. The pastern, however, can get lacerated. The wound can involve the horse's heel, and can even extend down to the coronary band. Avulsions, or wounds that include tearing away, happen more often in the hoof wall, usually at the quarter or heel. They can go up to the coronary band or down to the sole, as well.

Puncture wounds are the most common of all foot wounds affecting trail horses. Romeo once stepped on a pointed stick in such a way—I still don't know quite how he did it—that the tip got stuck in his coronary band and broke off. He stumbled right away, and when I got off, I could see the stick poking out of his foot. Fortunately, we were close to the barn, so I led him back, hobbling. The vet pulled out the stick and we were amazed at how long it was—about two inches. The resulting wound looked innocuous to me, but the vet said it was fairly serious, and I was lucky the stick had not punctured the synovial sac inside the foot. Romeo got antibiotics and rest, and was fine in a couple of weeks, but ever since then I'm wary whenever he takes a stumbling step.

Puncture wounds on the bottom of the horse's foot can be

difficult to see at first, since they only appear as a little dark spot on the sole. If a horse punctures his frog, the softer tissue there can even close over the puncture site, making it difficult to see. Since swift action is key to healing, if you know or suspect that your horse has a wound in his foot, presume that it's a serious injury until the vet arrives. If your horse won't put the injured foot on the ground, worry. If it turns out not to be serious, your speed in reacting can still alleviate pain, and if the injury is bad, and has contaminated a joint or sheath, then you have reduced a major threat to your horse's life with your attention.

When the vet arrives, she will probably use local anesthesia so she can explore the wound. She may use a tourniquet to look into the wound itself and see if any foreign object, such as a shard of glass, remains in the wound, and remove it. Romeo's vet used an x-ray to see how far the stick went into his foot. Some vets might inject fluid into the wound to see if it runs out through the wound. The only life-threatening news from a veterinarian's exam after a puncture wound is if the navicular or coffin bone has fractured into the joint, or if the joint or sheath are infected, but these are rare instances.

Vets differ on whether soaking helps a foot wound. Traditionally, equine health practitioners have horses stand with the injured foot in a bucket of water. Today, however, many vets say that soaking foot wounds is usually unnecessary, and may even cause damage to a deeper wound, since soaking can soften the hoof. Also, having the hoof alternately wet and then dried out, which is part of the nature of soaking, can stress it. Check with your vet, and follow her instructions. A poultice is more hygienic and can be applied for a longer period of time than standing a horse in a bucket. Gentle washing works well. You may have to learn new bandaging techniques, too, because foot wounds may require bandaging that involves layers of gauze, padding, and duct tape—to keep the bandage on as long as possible through a horse's stamping and itching.

# Eye Injury

Trail horses are vulnerable to eye injury because of their proximity to branches, cactuses, and gravel kicked up by their buddies or sand swirling on a windy day. Insects that fly into a horse's eye or sting him near it can also result in injured eyes.

Your main job is gently to take anything out—a pebble, a twig—that is hurting your horse. Next, decide if you believe the cornea has been scratched, in which case you will need to head home and call the vet right away. The cornea will appear white or grayish if it has been hurt. If he's in pain, your horse may refuse to open the eye, and if he has been kicked by another horse or if he has run into a branch or a trail sign, the eyelid may swell shut.

# Saddle Sores

Saddle sores are a common, but preventable, nuisance that can become a real problem if ignored. What may start as a minor problem caused by ill-fitting tack—it may just look like the hair is shorter where the girth or saddle has rubbed—can turn into an ugly blister. Feel where your horse's coat looks different, as you will be able to tell there is an inflamed area if a saddle sore is coming on. What happens is that skin cells die from too much pressure applied to a certain spot, and as they die, a sore forms. The withers and girth regions are, obviously, particularly at risk since that is where the most pressure from tack is.

Dirty or ill-fitting tack is at the root of this problem. Be sure that your horse's back and girth area are clean before you ride; your tack should be clean as well. A wrinkled saddle pad or a piece of leather or string caught under the pad can contribute to sores, too. Pine needles, leaves, or any debris from the trail that gets stuck to your horse can make a sore. Even a change in riders or the way in which you ride can also cause sores, because any change in pressure can make a difference. Wetness—if you get caught in the rain, or ford a high stream—causes a change in how things fit and rub (think about hiking in wet sneakers).

Changes in the horse's body weight—loss or gain—put him

Before you tighten the girth, be sure that the saddle is in the proper position. That way, you will avoid saddle sores.

at risk because he may not fit his tack any longer. Horses who are ribby may need extra padding to prevent their getting sores, and good saddle fit will often keep sores from developing in the first place.

If your horse gets a saddle sore, don't pile pads on him. It might seem like the horse would appreciate more cushioning, but the reverse is actually true. Although you want to keep the saddle off of the sore, the best way to do this is to cut an opening in one of your pads. The pad with the cutout will keep the saddle from touching the sore and release the pressure that caused the sore in the first place. Before you put the pad on, you might want to apply some petroleum jelly or an antibiotic ointment for further protection. And if you can, give your horse a rest until the sore heals.

One old trick to avoid sores concerns tacking up. Never slide your saddle forward. That will get the hair going the wrong way which could lead to a sore. Instead, place the saddle too far forward and allow it to slide back into position. The more you ride, the greater the likelihood for sores, which is why trail horses, who go so many miles, are particularly at risk for them.

# Poisonous Plants

We usually think of poisonous plants as a pasture danger. That's where horses are turned out, and that's where they can get into trouble by eating a lot of leaves from cherry trees, or onion grass. Horses are known to grab bites as they meander down the trail, and if you stop to picnic, your horse may eat on the road as well. It's important to know what poisonous plants are common in the area where you ride. If your horse's gums change color, his heart rate changes, or he gets severe diarrhea, suspect poisoning even if you can't imagine what toxic plants he could have been near.

Poisonous plants vary widely from region to region, which is why you should check with the county agricultural extension agent to get a list of them. Here are some of the most common and most toxic plants to horses:

Black Walnut Trees: The leaves, bark, and even some of the dirt around the base of the tree can carry the poison. Eating them can cause founder.

Onion Grass: If your horse smells like he has been snacking on onion rings, he has probably been into the onion grass. It is a particular problem in the early spring, since it comes in before many other grasses. Horses especially eager to see some grass start eating it in place of their usual diet. Onion grass can cause a bad form of anemia that can lead to red urine and profound fatigue.

Red Maple Trees: If ingested, the leaves, bark, or buds of a red maple tree can poison a horse. Like onion grass, red maple can make horses severely anemic. But it can also cause brown-colored blood and mucous membranes (lips, gums, etc.) from lack of oxygen.

Black cherry, wild cherry, chokecherry: If your horse grabs a few leaves from a cherry tree, don't worry too much. But once these leaves are crushed up, they release cyanide, which is as poisonous to horses as it is to us.

Oleander: Highly toxic to horses, who can die from eating the leaves.

Yew: Both Japanese and English varieties of this tree, which looks like a perfectly innocent evergreen, can kill a horse who just takes a few bites.

False Dandelion: This broadleaf, weedy-looking plant—*Hypochoeris radicata*—resembles the harmless dandelion, but if horses eat it it can cause them to get stringhalt, an evocatively named disease that causes lameness and a jerking motion, usually in the hind legs. You can recognize *Hypochoeris radicata* because although it seems to be a dandelion at first glance, each stem has more than one flower. Also, the petals are more daisylike.

## Snakebite

Snakes pose a threat because they can bite horses in the leg or muzzle. During night riding, snakes may be more prevalent since they tend to come out to enjoy the warm cement as the air cools. Snakes such as copperheads or water moccasins thrive in water and a horse may encounter them in creeks or streams. If you ride in an area where you know there are snakes, protective boots may be necessary for your horse.

When a horse gets bitten by a poisonous snake, its venom travels through the lymphatic system. The tissue right around the bite will die, and left untreated, the venom will make him sick or even cause death as it moves through his body.

If your horse gets bitten, keep him as quiet as possible, so that the venom will not move with such speed. If you have a snakebite kit with you (which is a good idea if poisonous snakes are a problem in your area), use the suction cups over the bite marks. Squeeze enough times to be sure you are removing poison from the site. Never apply a tourniquet to a snakebit horse, however. If you can, have the horse hauled home or to your vet right away. If you must lead him, do it slowly and with plenty of stops. Also, if you ride in a snakey area, you may want to carry a length of hose or tubing with you to open nasal passages in case they swell shut.

# Falls

If a rider falls on the trail, keep a few things in mind, especially if you are riding in a group. Have all the riders stop. (This is basic mannerly behavior if someone has fallen.) Then dismount and keep the rider still while you, or the most experienced person, checks for injuries. If the person is not conscious, send another rider to call 911, or use a cell phone to call.

If the person is unhurt, she is probably just embarrassed, so assure her that all riders fall. If she seems to be getting angry at her horse, try to prevent that by explaining the different things that probably contributed to the fall, from a startled horse to faulty equipment.

If you fall, try to think of what caused it. Did your horse spook and jump sideways? Were you unprepared when he hopped over a log instead of taking it in stride? Pause and take a moment after a fall, and if you need time to build your nerve back up, take it. If your fall happened when you were alone, the next time you

This rider is just pretending to be hurt, but if a rider is actually unconscious after a fall, get help right away.

ride, take a buddy with you. If staying in the arena makes you feel more secure, try that. If the accident happened on a new or borrowed horse, find an older or safer one to ride until you feel confident enough to take the one you rode when you fell.

## Runaway

Few things are more confidence-shattering than a runaway horse. When this happens in a group situation, the unfortunate rider is most likely embarrassed as well as terrified. To try to stop things from getting worse, keep your voice as level as possible and have the person circle. Often forcing a horse to make a circle, even at a gallop, will remind him who is supposed to be in control, and the circle gives rider and horse time to pull themselves together. If you need to go after the horse yourself, have someone turn to face the other riders so that their horses don't think that running away may, in fact, be a good idea.

Block the runaway horse's path if possible. Stand with your arms out to the sides for safety and to slow him down. But if trying to block his path may cause him to dart around you and run all the faster, let him go and continue asking the rider to circle and regain enough control to stop him.

If your horse gets out of control, there are a few ways to stop him. If he is not going too terribly fast, try to turn him in a circle or run him into a fence (unless you think he'll jump it). Riding with your reins bridged is a good idea if you're riding a horse who might get out of control. A pulley rein, in which you brace one of your hands against the horse's neck while lifting up with the other, also gives control. Also, when riding at speed, do half-halts every so often to remind your horse to listen to you. To do this, come into a three-point position (with three points of you touching the horse—your seat, your hands, and your heels) and open up your hips and put your shoulders back.

A horse that runs away often is not a good trail partner. He needs plenty of work in the ring and in other controlled environments before you take him out. Don't blindly follow advice about using a stronger bit; this is often ineffective and only makes the horse more sour and hostile toward you. If you're an experienced horseperson or your trainer recommends it, try a stronger bit for a horse that gets too strong, but don't depend solely upon that bit. Give your horse little "jobs" to do as you go down the trail—leg yields, halting and backing up—anything that keeps him tuned into you and what you are asking of him. That way, he will be less likely to tune you out when he decides to run.

Walk home. Nearly every horse picks up some speed as he senses he is heading back to the barn, some nice hay, and his friends. Resist the urge to let him canter back. He needs to cool down, for one thing. If you always walk, he'll realize that is the best way home. (And you will be surprised how springy and athletic his walk can be once he is finished working and heading home for the day.)

## Fatigue

Fatigue in horses can have several causes, including the dehydration and heat problems already discussed in this chapter. When your horse starts to stumble, breathe hard without stopping, and possibly even act grumpy, with pinned ears and a swishing tail, he may be getting tired. This is not an emergency unless you are so far away when exhaustion sets in that you can't ask your horse to continue on in the condition he's in. Lead him home slowly.

Once you get your horse back to the barn, make things easy on him. Give him his own paddock for a while if he usually gets run around by younger or more aggressive horses. A Vetrolin® bath will probably feel good, and he may need some ice or cold hosing on his legs, or even bute if you think he has aggravated any injuries or sore spots. Make sure he has all the water and salt he wants, and watch his urination and manure production.

Keeping him in shape and asking him to do tasks he is capable of will keep him from getting too tired. Weekend warrior horses suffer more from fatigue, because they are not worked during the week and then their riders take them on long, tiring rides. Try to give your horse moderate exercise so that he will be fit to carry you on a longer ride. And if you don't have a chance to

Letting a horse canter home is fun, but can lead to bad—and dangerous—habits.

ride as often as you'd like, don't ask your horse to do a great deal just because some time has opened up for you. Instead, take a shorter trail ride, or at least one on a loop that would allow you to go home earlier if you wanted to.

## Emergency Rescue

Sometimes a horse can be in great trouble on the trail. If, for example, he has fallen onto a ledge and can't climb up, the special equipment and expertise of an animal rescue team will be needed. Using a sling, a team can helicopter a hurt horse to a veterinary clinic. Plenty of phone calls to rangers and local authorities may be necessary to get the rescue team to the site. Keeping the horse as calm as possible while waiting for help to arrive is the main goal, along with explaining to contact people exactly where you and the downed horse are.

# Litters

If you have to carry a hurt rider out of a remote area, you will need to make a litter. Cavalry horses used to be trained in dragging litters to get wounded soldiers to the medics, but unless you have a very seasoned pack or driving horse along with you, your horse may not like this job, and the first time he drags a litter it should not be with an injured person at risk.

This leaves you and the other riders to bear the burden. Serious backpacking groups may carry a commercial litter for just such an eventuality, but you and your companions probably do not. The first thing you need to decide is if the injured person truly needs to get out of the woods right away, because getting medical help to the rider would be the safest course. In fact, attempting to evacuate the rider might pose a greater risk than staying put and waiting for help.

If, however, certain conditions are present—the person is unconscious, has difficulty breathing, or appears to be suffering from heatstroke or hypothermia (see Chapter 6)—then you need to get her out of the woods. You can fashion a litter from two long poles of dead wood and several shorter ones. Lay the shorter poles across the longer ones (like a ladder), and attach the shorter pieces to the longer ones with vines, spare lead ropes, or reins.

# 8 | Essential **Trail Gear**

Just as almost any horse can be a trail horse, almost all of your gear is already suitable for basic trail riding. You can head out in your jumping saddle or your roping one, your hackamore, double bridle, or halter-bridle. Unlike more formal riding sports, trail riding demands that more decisions be made about gear than attire. Getting your horse and yourself properly suited up will make for a more pleasant and safe trail riding experience.

## Helmets

Many trail riders do not wear helmets, rationalizing that because they are proceeding at a leisurely pace, nothing will happen. They are unwilling to tolerate the heat and weight of a helmet if it will mean sacrificing some comfort. Some Western riders are used to cowboy hats, and feel that helmets look silly.

Riding without a helmet is a mistake. Horseback riding, whether on a poky trail ride or racing, is dangerous, as is anything else that involves the possibility of a fall from a height. Head injury can be life-threatening. Helmets offer protection if your horse spooks and you fall off, or an unnoticed branch knocks you off your horse.

Consider the following facts from the American Medical Equestrian Association:

- Most riding injuries occur during pleasure riding.

- A fall from two feet can cause permanent brain damage, and a horse elevates a rider eight feet or more above ground.

- Helmets work. Most deaths from head injury can be prevented by wearing ASTM/SEI(American Society for Testing and Materials/Safety Equipment Institute)-approved helmets that fit correctly and have the chin strap firmly applied.

Also, with the technology that exists in helmets today, the excuses of being too hot or uncomfortable no longer hold true. There are helmets specifically made for trail riding or eventing. These new helmets focus on lightness and airflow, and some even have mesh under the ventilation holes to protect your head from falling leaves and branches. Many have removable visors to protect your face from sunburn.

Good fit is what makes your helmet effective, so take the time to find one that fits you well, and then adjust it properly. To check fit, rock the helmet backward and forward as well as side to side; your scalp should move with the helmet. Small fitting problems can be solved by using the foam padding that comes with the helmet, or by adjusting the internal harness. If the helmet needs more padding than is provided, or you just can't make it work, you need a smaller size or different model. Be sure to read the fitting instructions carefully and use all the fitting devices supplied with it—often straps, or Velcro pads, or a tightening dial. Professional help from someone at a tack store can be worth it, even if it costs a bit more to buy there than from a discounter. You're paying for the assistance, which can benefit you in the long run. Each helmet is different, and one you like the looks of may not fit you as well as another.

The rider on the bay is wearing a trail riding helmet with ventilation slots, while the rider on the chestnut is wearing a heavier, more traditional helmet. Both styles are effective if properly fitted.

Helmets made for trail riders are usually less expensive than velvet-covered helmets, and more sleekly designed. They look fine with Western or English turnout, but if you prefer a more traditional look, a helmet with a cowboy hat on top or a helmet designed to look like a hunt cap will do the trick. As long as a helmet is certified by a nationally recognized safety board, such as ASTM/SEI or BETA (British Equestrian Trade Association), it will offer your head protection whenever you ride.

A helmet that has been in a hard fall should be inspected by the manufacturer or replaced. If you're wondering if your helmet needs to be replaced after a fall, look for these defects: harness pulling loose from the helmet; clips with broken teeth; surface cracks, holes, or dents; material missing from the liner; and a cracked shell. Whenever you buy a new helmet, keep your receipt. Many companies have replacement policies and if you have proof of purchase, you can obtain a new helmet at a reduced price if the original helmet is damaged.

## Gloves

Even if you don't normally wear gloves when riding, you may want some with you when you are trail riding. If you need to move brush or deal with muddy feet, you will be glad you have some protection for your hands. Keep gloves in your pommel bag if you don't want to wear them.

## Fly Protection

Insects are a summertime nuisance for any rider, but they plague trail riders in particular. Buggy woods and fields hazed with gnats are annoying enough, but it is downright scary to be riding along and have a horsefly bite your horse—or you. A horsefly sting hurts, and can cause a horse to bolt from the pain and surprise. Insects will be less of a bother and your trail ride will be more pleasant if you take precautions.

Crocheted ear nets are one way to keep bugs off of your horse's sensitive ears. These nets cover his ears, and because they have tassels that hang down in front of his forelock, their motion waves flies away.

You're used to seeing fly masks on turned-out horses, but masks are made for horses under saddle as well. Just like the

A crocheted ear net keeps biting insects away from a horse's sensitive ears.

pasture versions, these are of a see-through mesh. Horses can see out, but bugs cannot get in. Suits made of this mesh are available for riders, and leggings called "fly boots" are highly effective in protecting horses' legs but take some getting used to. Horses who are already turned out in masks do particularly well in the under-saddle versions.

Apply fly spray before you leave the barn. The active ingredient in fly sprays is typically pyrethrin, which is derived from chrysanthemums, or a synthetic version called a pyrethoid. These sprays kill flies as well as repel them. You can buy "natural" fly control products that work by masking the horse's scent to insects, and these usually contain cedar or citronella oil. When trail riding, unless you are very opposed to using chemicals on your horse, old-fashioned fly spray with a pyrethrin or pyrethroid is the best bet, and one with an oil base rather than a water base is longer lasting. Repellents lack the staying power and effectiveness of insecticides, although they may be more pleasant to smell.

Even though you apply fly spray at the barn before you leave, it's best to carry more with you, either in a roll-on or gel form. Sweat causes fly spray to wear off, and having more protection in a concentrated form allows you to reapply it around your horse's eyes and ears to minimize headshaking as you ride along.

A fly whisk lets you help keep flies from landing on your horse.

Spot-on insecticides are available, too. These, like many fly sprays, use pyrethrin or a pyrethroid. They require application every two weeks instead of every day, and work well for the trail horse because they offer a low-maintenance way to keep flies at bay. The only problem is that you cannot bathe your horse with traditional soap while he is being treated with a spot-on insecticide, so you have to buy the special shampoo that allows it to remain effective even after a bath, which most horses will need after a summertime trail ride.

An old-fashioned way to control flies is with a fly whisk. You hold a wooden handle and ride along shooing flies from your horse's head and neck with a "tail" at the end. It has the same effect as when your horse and a buddy stand head to tail in the pasture, swishing flies. Obviously, a fly whisk is best used on a very lazy trail ride, not on a day when you are trying to trot a lot or work on bombproofing.

## Clothes

Any tack store employee will have a story about someone who came in to be outfitted for a first riding lesson, and wanted to wear a shadbelly, tall boots, and a bowler. Or the foxhunting neophyte who thinks he has to wear the old style of puffed-thigh jodhpurs and carry the horn himself. Trail riding is nice in that it does not invite ridiculous affectation. You can wear the least formal version of whatever your discipline requires. English riders often take to the trail in schooling chaps, paddock boots, and a helmet, while many English and Western riders alike forego the chaps altogether and just set out in jeans and boots. Endurance riders have their own look, which is still much less proscribed than that of other equestrian sports. They usually wear ventilated trail helmets, and many of them wear half-chaps over stretch breeches or jods. Anything goes. The key is that you feel comfortable and are safe. Sneakers are as dangerous on the trail as in the ring; your feet can still slide through the stirrup.

Chaps can be wonderful on the trail, because they protect your legs from scratchy bushes and trees as well as adding contact

between legs and saddle. Show chaps are sometimes less than useful, though. You worry about them getting scratched, which defeats their purpose. Either use your older pair of schooling chaps for the trail, or buy a looser fitting pair of off-the-rack chaps to be your "trail chaps" and save your good ones for schooling or show.

Casual is the mode for trail ride dress; many riders just wear jeans. Kneesocks underneath ensure a minimum of stirrup leather rubs. Khakis and shorts are both out because they allow rubbing, especially at the slower trail riding gaits of walking and trotting. English riders may prefer to wear a pair of jodhpurs or breeches, because the stretchy fabric is comfortable for a long ride.

"Riding tights," like breeches and jods, are close fitting and stretchy, and usually made with Lycra or other shape-holding fabric. They look more like athletic tights, except that they usually have a knee patch and they come in all sorts of colors and patterns. Leggings, tall boots, or half-chaps can also provide calf protection for people riding in tights, breeches, or jodhpurs. The nice thing about breeches, jods, or tights instead of jeans is that you don't

need the socks underneath to protect from chafing. Usually, since the fabric is so close-fitting, it won't rub on your calf even as you post at the trot.

## Footwear

Paddock boots are often the trail rider's choice, as tall boots tend to get scratched or wet more on the trail than is cost-effective. Also, tall boots may not be comfortable for long hours of riding. Paddock boots give you all-in-one protection for your lower leg and foot, as do cowboy boots.

The riding sneaker is the newest addition to equestrian footwear. Although traditionalists may be appalled at them, they have a place for trail riders. They resemble hiking boots, but have a smoother sole and a good-sized heel. Riding sneakers are lighter in weight than riding boots, and are specifically constructed for riding, unlike regular sneakers.

Remember that any time you head out for a trail ride, there is a chance you will be walking back. If your horse pulls up lame, you will need to hop off and lead him home. So make sure your riding boots are comfortable to walk in. Endurance riders often ride in sneakers or tennis shoes, which is not necessarily the safest plan, but it works for them because they spend so much time on the ground between vet checks and "tailing" their horses. (Endurance riders often use safety stirrups, so even in sneakers, their feet won't fly through the stirrups.)

## Cameras

You may want to carry a camera with you on the trail, but it's not easy to take care of it as you ride. One solution is to carry a disposable camera in your pack or pocket, but if you take a "real" camera with you, you may want to wear one of those safari/photographer's vests so that it you don't risk dropping it. A camera case is too unwieldy, and a backpack big enough for a camera and photographic gear will not be safe either. Instead, try a small digital or film camera that you can put in a pommel or cantle bag, saddle pad, vest or jacket pocket.

## Packs

Real horse campers and people out for long rides use pack horses or mules. These animals carry specially designed packs that contain food, tents, and equipment for the trip. For most trail riders, however, a pack horse is unnecessary. But you will want to carry more stuff with you than you do when you're working in the ring. You want to bring your camera, cell phone, trail map, energy bar, water bottle, first-aid kit, Easyboot . . . it gets to be a long list. So although you don't need a separate pack horse, you do need to turn your own horse into sort of a pack animal.

As you would expect, a pommel bag goes on the front of your saddle, and a cantle bag goes on the back. Bags are made of leather, cotton duck, or another durable material, and are attached to the dee rings with clips or string. If you're a parent, this bag is the equivalent of your diaper bag, because it has things for emergencies and things for convenience.

What goes in is a personal choice, of course, but there are

A cantle bag is big enough to hold essentials like a first-aid kit, hoofpick, and map.

items that you should carry. A folding hoofpick and first-aid kit belong in your cantle or pommel bag, as well as your GPS or compass. Your Easyboot and some Vetrap™ can go in here as well for emergencies. A small human first-aid kit is a good idea along with your equine one. You never know when you will be happy to have gauze, acetaminophen, or even just a Band-Aid. Water and a couple of energy bars are a good idea always to keep on hand as well. A special pocketknife made for riders that has a folding hoof-pick as well as blades sharp enough for cutting reins in an emergency is a convenient option.

You may be tempted to bear the burden yourself and put these items into a backpack. It is doable on horseback, but not much fun. Unless it is perfectly balanced and fitted, a backpack tends to swing around as you ride. This is unpleasant at best and at worst can annoy your horse. It's also bad for your riding position, because wearing a backpack will make you hunch over, and you may find yourself coming home much more sore than a trail ride should have left you.

Many riders like fanny packs. Because they go around your waist, they are less likely to cause an imbalance. But they can be cumbersome, and can flap around if you are riding at speed. If you decide to use one, use it for Band-Aids, one or two keys, or cash for the vending machines at the park. Even a cell phone will slam around unpleasantly in a fanny pack.

## Saddles

Just as in other horse sports, riders should buy the best leather goods they can afford. Although good tack may seem prohibitively expensive, it pays for itself in the long run since it does not need to be replaced as often as cheaper tack does. Look for leather made in England, Canada, Germany or the United States. Also look for vegetable-tanned leather. Anything that has a chemical smell, or an acidic one, is probably not vegetable tanned. Trust yourself: good leather has a sweet, clean, "tack shop" smell to it. Saddles and bridles should have strong, clean stitching and the leather itself should have a uniform look to it. High-quality leather should glow.

If you're trying to save money, consider shopping for used tack at your local tack store. Older leather, like newer leather, should have a good, leathery smell. It should not have abrasions or marks on it, and the edges of reins, leathers and billets should be finished rather than rough. It should be pliant and not wrinkly. Check stitching and straps before you buy used tack. It can be very discouraging to try to restore low-quality leather. Cheap leather cracks more easily, is not as resilient, and stains more easily than its more expensive and higher-quality counterpart, so whether the leather you're buying is new or old, verify that it is high quality.

Saddle fit is a more important concern than saddle age, since both new and used saddles can achieve the desired fit on your horse's back. In fact, riders on a budget should look for an older, quality-made used saddle rather than settle for a cheap brand, which may be poorly made and less likely to fit. No one saddle or brand will solve everyone's saddle fitting needs. Custom saddles are a possibility, of course, but are usually prohibitively expensive for many trail riders.

Another option is buying synthetic. Synthetic saddles don't spend too much time in the show ring because their appearance is not as elegant as that of leather, but they are a wonderful choice for trail riders since they are economical and require almost no care. They can get soaking wet without your having to spend hours cleaning and reconditioning them when you get back to the barn. They're lightweight, and don't deteriorate with age or get moldy the way leather can.

A well-fitted saddle will allow your horse to carry you more easily and comfortably for longer. If you suspect back problems or are seeking ways to improve your horse's poor performance, saddle fit may be an issue. Where the saddle bears down and how it distributes the weight of carrying a rider in motion as well as standing still are what decides how the horse feels, which in turn affects his health and your ride.

Uneven pressure is difficult for a horse to carry, as is concentrated and immobile pressure. In extreme cases, it's pressure that causes the white hair scars that tell on an ill-fitting saddle. If you're trying to decide whether a saddle you already own fits, listen to your horse because he will be the first to tell you if he's in pain. Look at his back when you are through riding for the day. Hair forced the wrong way back by the panel may mean that the saddle was shifting and rubbing as you rode.

If he seems constantly stiff or cold-backed, or has white hair scars on his withers or spine, an ill-fitting saddle may be the cause. Head-tossing or shortening of strides may also be an indication that his back hurts, which could also suggest a possible saddle fit problem.

To evaluate saddle fit, look at the horse's back from the front, from the sides, and from above. Stand your horse on a level surface before you tack up so that uneven ground doesn't interfere with fit. As you saddle up, resist the temptation to put your saddle up on your horse's withers. English and Western riders alike have a tendency to put their saddles too far forward. The saddle should be behind the shoulders so that the horse can move freely. Start with your saddle forward, and slowly slide it back until it stops. It should almost feel as if it has "clicked" into place, which should help prevent saddle sores as well as improve fit.

Once the saddle is on the horse's back, look across the front of the saddle; it should be the same distance above the skin all the way across. You should be able to get two or three fingers between the saddle's pommel and the horse's withers to ensure that the saddle is not pressing on him. You should only be able to see a little daylight underneath the saddle from the front to the back.

The cantle should be higher than the pommel, and when you press down on the pommel, the cantle should not pop up. If it does, it means the saddle "rocks." Because the rocking motion presses on the horse's back, it will cause pain as he moves. On a long trail ride, this pressure will be exacerbated with each mile. When you stand behind your horse, you should see that the shape of the arch of the panel is the same all the way across, with the whole panel touching the horse. When it doesn't all touch, it means that the saddle is "bridging," or allowing a gap that in turn creates pressure points on the horse. The saddle should be level from side to side and carry the rider naturally in its deepest part. The rider should not feel as though she is riding up or down hill.

The tree of the saddle should be parallel to the horse's withers. This can be difficult to determine, however. The cantle-pommel relationship can give you hints about the tree. If the cantle is lower than the pommel, and there is too much clearance under the pommel, you should consider a narrower tree. If the cantle is higher and there is not enough room between withers and pommel, you may need a wider tree.

If your English saddle is not fitting correctly after years of

The fit of the saddle is more important than style or size. This stock saddle seems to fit the horse well.

satisfactory use, don't give up on it. You may be able to get much more time out of that saddle by having its panels restuffed or reflocked, which is the process of replacing the filling. There's no difference between "restuffing" and "reflocking," but the former is the more common term. Saddlers unstitch the panels, remove the old stuffing (typically wool, polyester, or a mix), and replace it with fresh filling material.

Restuffing may also be a solution for an older saddle if the bottoms of the panels are lumpy, if there is a hollow spot, or if there are bumpy places. Panels that feel hard or have valleys may need some work. Your saddle will need restuffing if you suddenly find that you're too far behind or in front of the motion even though you have not changed your riding at all. "Rocking" is a further indication that a saddle needs restuffing. Stuffing will start to build in various places, and that will make the panels look like they are rocking. When a saddle starts to get low and rock, it will cause a lump under the cantle right where the leg comes off of the seat. The saddle may tip forward or backward, and if your horse is getting pinched at the shoulder area, and he won't give you his back, it might be time to check your saddle.

## Children's Gear

Children's trail riding gear is similar to what adults use. A saddle should fit the child's mount well, be comfortable for the child, and ideally be easy to care for. As cozy as it seems to ride double with your little trail rider, it's an unsafe practice. Despite there being gadgets that make it easy to do so, like stirrups that go over the saddle horn and double pads, duplex saddles, and similar systems, riding double is a bad idea. Children are ready for their own saddles when they are no longer being led and can steer a horse by themselves.

Saddle fit is as important for children's mounts as for adults, as is stirrup safety. If the stirrup leathers are set on very deep bars or on a non-release bar, you need safety stirrups, which children should have anyway. Western saddles work well for small children who might want to grab the horn at times, and some English lead-line models have a pommel or buck strap that children can grab instead of their horse's mane. Many English saddles are made on wider trees to fit the chubby ponies children are likely to ride.

## Caring for Tack

Now that you have all this expensive tack, how do you make it last? There are so many different rules about leather care that if you try to follow them all, they begin to cancel each other out. Frustration may set in before you even begin. Then you'll neglect your tack, which results in the worst possible scenario: dirty, unsafe leather equipment. Leather care methods will vary, depending upon the condition of the leather and what you are trying to accomplish.

The point is to make sure that your tack is clean and conditioned. Without proper care, saddles and bridles will dry out and crack, or if they are too damp, will get moldy. Regular cleaning and conditioning will prevent this from happening, and your tack will reward you with years of service and good looks. A good saddle will last a lifetime if you take care of it.

Each time you ride your tack gets grimy. If you get caught in a downpour during a trail ride, there is not too much you can do about your saddle getting soaked. Sweat, water, and dirt are all enemies of leather. Leather consists of layers. The top layer, or grain, is the outermost surface of the animal's skin. It has pores, which maintained the original animal's fluid balance. Once tanned, these pores absorb the oil and conditioner you apply. The next layer is the fibrous, interlocking corium, which is the fundamental structure of the leather. The corium is most of the leather's bulk, and is well protected by being the central layer. It needs conditioning so that the interlocking fibers, which continually rub against each other, do not erode. The bottom layer is called the rough. (You may have chaps that are called rough-outs for their suedelike surface.) The rough is the most absorbent and least finished side of the leather.

Your tack should not be kept in a place that is damp, because it can get mildewed, and a place that is too hot will cause it to crack. A tack room should be dry and not have the extremes in temperature that the rest of the barn may. Keep your saddle covered to protect it from exposure, as well as unsightly scratches from the barn cats or teeth marks from mice.

Cleanliness preserves tack. You can get away with wiping it down daily with a damp cloth when you get home from your ride, but every once in a while—once a week, if you ride every day—you should really clean your tack. This includes soaping it, as well as conditioning and sealing it if necessary. Caring for your tack also gives you an opportunity to look for the wear that can cause unsafe riding, like loose or frayed stitching that could cause a girth or bridle to slip. Your saddle's billets should be strong and well-stitched, with appropriately sized holes and no weak spots with creases. Look at your keepers and stirrup leathers to be sure that they, too, are whole and strong. Tack can weaken even when it is just sitting in the tack room or in your trailer, so check any equipment before you go riding in it.

## How to Clean Tack

Get yourself set up with a rag, water, and all your cleaning supplies. A saddle rack at a sink works perfectly, but a chair back and a bowl of water will do as well. Take your stirrups off your saddle, and take your bridle apart. To make them easier to scrub later, allow your bit and stirrup irons to soak in warm water while you do the rest of the cleaning.

Check the integrity of metal pieces like the safety bars under the saddle's skirts. Some metals that come into contact with leather and leather preservatives turn black or get green gunk on them, which should come off with elbow grease and maybe a little metal polish. Clean any dirty metal bits first, since it's hard to keep the metal cleaner from getting on the leather. Once you've polished the metal bits, wipe any excess metal polish off surrounding leather so it doesn't stain.

Wipe your whole saddle and bridle down with a damp (not wet) sponge or cloth. Terrycloth, such as rags cut from an old towel or an inside-out old athletic sock, works well. Lather your tack with saddle soap next, applying the soap in a circular motion,

Clean tack not only makes for more attractive turnout, but also is better for your horse since it won't trap dirt and irritate his skin.

and working between the crevices and any tooling. As you wash, keep rinsing out your sponge and when you finish, make sure no soap is left on the leather. Once you have finished with the top side of the saddle, flip it over and clean the flaps, both sides of the sweat flaps, panel, gullet liner and knee rolls. Remember, the underside is closest to the sweat and dirt from your horse, so it needs special attention even though it's not visible.

Get rid of all the jockeys, which are the black, gummy spots of grime that stick to leather. You need to really work to remove them, so use an old toothbrush or even very fine steel wool, if necessary. Jockeys can be frustratingly hard to remove sometimes, but don't use harsh cleaners even if people at the barn recommend them. Any caustic cleaning solution, like most detergents, ammonia, and bleach, can dry out and discolor leather. So no matter how filthy your tack, only use gentle products and hard work. Your tack should be damp when you're finished. Always allow it to dry naturally before you condition it. It's not necessary to condition tack each time you clean it, however.

# Conditioning and Sealing Tack

A leather conditioner replaces the fat and oil that get lost in the natural course of using tack, and works the same way that a moisturizing lotion works on skin. How often you need to condition your tack depends upon many factors, such as where you live and how often you ride. Tack that has gotten totally drenched will need to be conditioned even if it has just been done recently.

Well-conditioned leather will look and feel even in texture and tone. It should shine. You can choose from the countless conditioners on the market, or use various oils—olive, neat's-foot, and vegetable among them. Conditioners typically are based on a fat (animal or vegetable), and have various additives. Old-fashioned neat's-foot oil used to be viewed as a cure-all for leather, but now many people mistakenly steer clear of it. That's because over the years, many neat's-foot oil producers began adding other ingredients to the oil, compromising its effectiveness. Neat's-foot oil compounds have harsh petroleum products and should not be used on leather, but regular old-fashioned neat's-foot oil (which is usually what you'll find in a tack or feed store) is fine.

Condition your tack when the leather starts looking dry. Your saddle is ready to be conditioned—or "dressed"—when it is very clean and nearly dry. To apply oil, soak a soft cloth and lightly oil the tack all over, then resoak the cloth whenever it starts to seem dry. Or use a brush. Keep oil away from suede knee rolls, or other suede components your saddle may have, because it will stain. Apply a second light coat rather than over-soaking the leather the first time around. Over-oiling will make your tack feel floppy, which in turn compromises the strength and thus the safety of your equipment. The same goes for creamier conditioners.

For tack that has been water-soaked or just really needs deep conditioning, dip it into a pan of oil. Wipe the leather down as soon as you remove it from the oil, and don't ever dip your whole saddle, because the oil can get into the stuffing inside.

Sealing tack is a good idea for trail equipment which is prone to getting soaked. When leather gets wet, water forms a temporary bond with the oils lubricating the leather's fibers and washes them away. This leaves tack more vulnerable to scarring because the protein bonds holding the leather fibers together break more easily, making the leather stiffer. Tack should be well-oiled and conditioned before you seal it, because you won't be able to add more conditioner once it is sealed. Then the next time you give your tack a deep cleaning, re-washing and conditioning the leather, you will remove the seal.

You can seal leather with glycerin soap. Rub a bar of soap—wet, but not so wet it will lather—all over the tack. Wipe it down with a clean rag so you can see that it is coating the tack evenly. An alternate method is to use a damp cloth and either a liquid or solid form of glycerin. Apply the soap, and then rub until your leather has a smooth, low-light sheen to it. Then, every time you ride, wipe your saddle off with a clean damp sponge to remove dirt.

Any feed or tack store will have plenty of products guaranteed to make your tack water-resistant. Silicone sprays repel water, which can make the leather's surface feel a little slippery, so don't use silicone on reins. Acrylic copolymer sprays work especially well on suede. They leave a protective coating that protects the leather from rain while maintaining the leather's ability to breathe. Follow the instructions on any product's label, and be sure that the leather is not wet when you seal it, because sealing wet leather can lead to mildew.

Tack stored somewhere humid or airless can get moldy, leaving unsightly streaks and patches on the leather. Avoid putting your wet saddle pad over your saddle, and if you begin to see signs of mold, invest in some dehumidifiers or fans for the tack storage area. If you see mold on your tack, you can clean it off with white vinegar. Do not use bleach. Just coat your tack with the vinegar, and give it about four to six hours to work. Then wipe it off, and clean and condition as usual. If the mold has really settled in, use very fine (0000) steel wool to remove the greenish spots.

## Caring for Boots and Chaps

Trail riders are hard on their own clothes as well as their gear, and fortified boots and chaps will be less likely to scratch and fray if they are kept clean and conditioned. Boot dryers can be helpful for boots that get damp and dirty often. Follow tack cleaning instructions to get this gear in shape—clean thoroughly, don't over-oil, and seal or waterproof if you like. For boots made of suede or that have other rough finishes, remove loose dirt or dust with a brush or rag and brush clean.

The best way to clean chaps is to have them professionally dry-cleaned by a firm that specializes in cleaning leather. A shopping center close to a horsey area will usually have such a store. The dry cleaner will add conditioners to keep chaps supple and looking good. To clean suede chaps yourself, brush them regularly with a suede brush. Chaps can occasionally be washed at home in a washing machine, on the gentle cycle, with a mild detergent or one designed for leathers. Chaps can even be put in the dryer, if yours has a cycle without heat. Use a dryer sheet, and pull the chaps out when they are still a bit damp so that they can be stretched to their original shape and laid flat to dry. If your chaps are off-the-rack, follow manufacturer's instructions for cleaning.

Having synthetic tack alleviates much of the concern about conditioning, since synthetic material does not require anywhere near the amount of care that leather does. Just gentle dishwashing soap and water will be fine. The only product to avoid is glycerin saddle soap, which will leave a residue since the synthetic material cannot absorb it. It used to be a bad idea to mix real leather with synthetic (for example, using leather stirrup leathers on a synthetic saddle) because the oils on the natural leather could weaken the synthetic material, but it is no longer because the materials have been improved.

## Saddle Pads

In the past, many riders did not even use saddle pads at all, and today some riders still swear by padless riding as the best way to break in a new saddle. But many of us like saddle pads for their various colors and patterns, as well as the way they look on our horses. Trail riders like pads with pockets that are thick enough to cushion the horse's back, but thin enough not to interfere with the way a good saddle fits.

But too many riders depend upon their pads to perform miracles. Even the most amazing pad cannot fix an ill-fitting saddle, and any saddle should fit well enough not to require therapeutic pads. Some pads, however, can help horses who are experiencing changes in muscle or weight. When an owner simply can't afford to change saddles and has to make do with one that doesn't fit her horse perfectly, then a therapeutic pad can help. Therapeutic pads can be very expensive, so restuffing a saddle might be a more cost-effective way to ameliorate fit without resorting to padding.

Saddle pad shape is everything. Most trail riders depend upon square pads—and more of them come with pockets, which are a wonderful advantage for trail riders—but a shaped, jumper-style pad is fine as well. Square pads are the most common under-saddle items on the trail. Once you've put a pad on correctly—avoiding potential pressure on the withers by pushing the front of the saddle pad up under the pommel, creating a "vent" that will allow some air flow and less force as you ride—all you have to do is choose the color. Baby pads or underpads, the thin cotton versions of regular pads, are ideal in the blazing heat of the summer if you want to wash the heavier pads less frequently or if you like to use a cotton pad underneath a therapeutic pad. If

A saddle pad with pockets is ideal for trail riders, because it eliminates the need for pommel or cantle bags, yet allows you to store some equipment.

your horse gets very sweaty and dirty on the trail, it's nice to be able to throw a lightweight baby pad in the wash every day instead of a big heavy trail pad. Even the most inexpensive square pads now come in contoured versions, which just means there is more room for the horse's withers. These pop up a bit in front and form a V-shape, as if you had already created the vent.

Trail riders may use more serious shape-changing pads if they have a very specific saddle fit problem, or have so many horses that pads are the only way to keep them all even marginally comfortable in the same saddle. These include wedge pads, which increase in height from the front to the back of the pad. These help level a saddle, which can assist a horse with sensitive spine areas. Wedge-shaped pads decrease in height from the back to the front of the pad, which helps keep saddles back. A keyhole pad pushes the rider forward, and a lollipop pad will usually provide lift toward the pommel. Bump pads and riser pads lift the cantle. Cutback or cutout pads work by removing the parts of a pad that could cause pressure and pain over sensitive places.

Non-slip pads help trail riders, who may find that their saddles shift and shimmy over a long day on the trail. Some riders use breast collars to keep their saddles steady, but these pads will help, too. A horse whose deepest part is directly behind his elbow, for example, may be more inclined to have a slipping saddle. A chamois cloth placed on top of a regular pad and toward the pommel is an old-fashioned and effective way of stopping saddle slide.

Saddle pads made of new materials seem to appear on the market every day. Any padding that can sustain pressure and act as a barrier between saddle and horse has been used to make a saddle pad, including varieties of foam and gel, as well as natural materials like wool or fleece. Combinations like a foam pad with a wool cover or a quilted cotton pad with fleece on the reverse side are available as well. It's convenient if the pad comes with a removable cover. Then you can take out the cushioning material and wash the pad so that the part next to the horse can be kept clean.

Gel pads often come with covers. Some of these pads are filled with gel all the way through, and others have two distinct gel pockets that lie along the horse's spine on either side so the gel won't press on the spine. Gel pads work especially well beneath jumping saddles with flat panels with little flocking in them, because the gel acts as the replacement for the missing wool or cushioning. If you're a jumper rider trying to make your saddle work for long trail rides, a gel pad may offer comfort.

If you are into magnetic therapy for yourself or your horse, you might want a magnetic pad. No one really knows how or why magnets work as pain relievers, but for those who like them, the saddle pads apply magnetic fields to the most pressure-filled parts of a horse's back.

The "old-school" type of pad to use for any kind of distance riding is wool. You can't go wrong with this traditional material, and many pads have wool on the underside, even if the rest of the pad is made of something else. Wool wicks moisture away from the horse and insulates against both cold and heat, and because wool pads don't shift, they are ideal for trail riding.

Like wool, fleece has natural advantages for trail riders. Real wool fleece is more absorbent than the synthetic kind, but some horses are allergic to the latter. Fleece, whether natural or polyester, provides all-around cushioning. Some people swear by real sheepskin, which is expensive, but beautiful and also very absorbent. It is really tough to clean, a disadvantage that makes synthetic sheepskin a viable option. There are two types of foam pads: closed and open cell. Closed-cell foam pads cushion without collapsing and are very durable. They look more like flexible styrofoam. Open-cell foam pads are very thin and recover well from pressure, like football padding.

Use one pad at a time, because as you start stacking you dramatically change the fit of the saddle, since extra pads tend to raise the front. Also, too much padding distances you from your horse right when you need to be able to communicate with him as he mounts a hill or steps through a stream.

## Safety Stirrups

Don't think of safety stirrups as a kid's precaution; they are important for trail riders of any age. They are designed to protect you from being dragged in the event of a fall. If you're riding in traditional Fillis irons or Western stirrups when you fall, there's always a chance that your foot will go through the stirrup and get caught at the ankle, and then you will be dragged along the ground behind your galloping horse.

As safety stirrups become more and more common, people will be less and less self-conscious about them. But traditionalists—especially those who spend a lot of time in the show ring—may prefer those stirrups that mimic a traditional Fillis iron most closely. Trail riders have no such excuse and should ride in safeties all the time.

Safety stirrups basically come in two varieties: those that work because of their unusual shape, and those that work because of their inner mechanisms. Some people prefer a release mechanism that they can see, such as a side that hinges out or an elastic band in place of steel. Some like the stirrups that are shaped so that a foot can slide out, since these do not have moving parts that can squeak, feel unstable, or otherwise make their presence known while riding.

The appearance-conscious rider should know that almost all safety stirrups look quite different from standard irons. Many people think "peacock" when they hear "safety stirrup." Some may feel less secure knowing that the outside of their foot has only a rubber band to support it. On the flip side, you can be confident that an elastic band will pop off in the event your foot gets caught. But since you shouldn't be leaning on that outer part of the stirrup anyway, peacocks are fine. They are almost always the cheapest way to go, and are perfect for adult beginners who need a safety stirrup but are not sure they'll stay in the sport, or for children who will just need a bigger size next year anyway, and whose weight might not be enough to bring the stirrup leather off safety bar.

Peacock stirrup elastics come in black and dark brown, which makes them less conspicuous, but harder to find if they come off and fall onto the trail. Peacocks are traditionally used on children's saddles, so some adults may feel a little silly riding in them. Also, the elastics will occasionally pop off, so take some spares with you on a long trail ride. When you are mounting, make sure your foot is not too far over when you spring up, because the elastic can pop off and you will have to get down, grovel for the elastic in the dirt, and start all over again.

If you want to avoid mechanisms entirely, buy a shaped safety stirrup. These work by allowing the foot to slide out, which it can do because the stirrup has enough room. Once you get used to the sensation of the bar near your little toe, it is comfortable. These stirrups are a good choice if you are resistant to changing the ones you've always ridden in, but want added safety.

If you still don't want to ride in a pair of safety stirrups, you can make your regular irons as safe as possible. Leave your stirrup bars in an open position, and buy stirrups that fit your feet. The width of the tread of the stirrup should be ½ to ¾ inches wider than the width of the boot at the ball of the foot. Measure your foot at the widest part, and that number will give you your stirrup size.

## Halter-bridles

You never see halter-bridles in the show ring, because they look a little bit like a homemade contraption. But halter-bridles can be lifesavers on the trail. A halter-bridle is a piece of equipment that can act as a halter, which provides a place to secure a horse, and a bridle, which includes a bit and allows you to guide your horse from his back.

A halter-bridle allows you to take the horse's bit out of his mouth without removing the whole thing. So you can untack your horse while he is tied, without even that brief moment that he usually stands in the cross-ties "naked," after you have shucked the bridle off but before you have put the halter back on. It's very nice to be able to do this when you're on the trail stopping for a picnic or dismounting briefly.

The typical halter-bridle looks like a halter with reins, except that it has more snaps to connect pieces. Others look more like bridles, complete with browband. You pop the bit off by means of a snap attaching to the cheekpieces.

Just as you never tie a horse by his reins in a regular bridle, don't get lazy and try it with a halter-bridle. You need to disassemble it before you can secure your horse.

## Seat Savers

As you probably know after your first trail ride after some time off, your seat can suffer considerably while riding long miles at fairly slow paces. Trotting can alleviate this problem, but for some people, trail riding necessarily means a sore rear end. The soreness may go away as you ride more and more, but if it does not let up, it can make trail riding more of a chore than a pleasure.

There are a few ways to tackle this problem. One way is with a seat saver made of sheepskin or other cushiony fabric. The idea is to make your saddle softer so that your seat bones do not slam on a hard saddle, but on a pillowy base. A seat saver may look a bit cumbersome but it really helps people who otherwise get sore.

Another way is by wearing padded breeches or underwear. This is one instance where you need to stick with equestrian retailers; buying padded seat underwear from a cycling company may put the padding in the wrong place and not help you.

The best way to keep your lower back healthy is with exercise and stretching, but since lower back pain can be brought on by stress such as riding, a seat saver may help this problem. Lower back pain can be alleviated, some say, with a therapeutic seat saver.

## Shoeing

Technically speaking, horseshoes are not considered trail gear, because all horse owners have to decide whether or not to use shoes, but trail riding brings with it its own set of shoeing concerns. If you have ridden your horse in a sand arena for many years, when you start riding on trails you may find that he gets tender-footed. You may see him jerk up his feet, or otherwise favor his feet, which may be getting bruised from the unaccustomed terrain. He may need to be shod up front, at least.

At the other end of the spectrum are hard-footed horses who don't need shoes at all. These fortunate souls are sound no matter the footing. There are many things that affect hoof quality, from nutrition to footing to farriery, so your farrier is the best person to ask about your horse's shoeing needs. Remember that even a bare-

foot horse has to be trimmed by the farrier every six weeks or so. Many trail horses only have shoes on their front feet, which is also desirable on horses who are turned out, since it lessens the chance that they will hurt a pasture mate with a flying rear kick.

Corrective shoeing can help trail horses. Horses who tend to stumble, for example, benefit from having their toes rolled. This means that the farrier rounds the shoe up a bit up front, so that the horse breaks over more easily. This lessens tripping. Quarter or toe clips help shoes stay on, which can be a real benefit for trail riders who experience muddy or wet conditions frequently.

Some trail riders use permanent calks on their horses' shoes. These protrusions help the horse to grab the turf as he moves. They are not quite as protuberant as screw-in calks, which can be worn by horses in icy conditions.

## Spurs

For the most part, spurs don't have a place in trail riding. Big, long spurs are a bad idea in the woods because branches catch on them and press them into your horse. Otherwise, unless your horse is so balky that you have found spurs the only way to urge him on, you should not need spurs when you're out to enjoy a trail ride. And only very experienced riders should use them, because they can make a horse dead to the aids and sullen if used improperly or too much.

## Trail Bell

Horse packers use bells to know where their horses are in a field at night. Now, some trail riders are starting to use them as well. Bells can attach to the breast collar, girth, or the bridle, and serve the same function as bicycle bells: to alert others on the trail of the rider's presence. They are much softer than bicycle bells, but horses have to get used to them, both on themselves and on other horses.

## Bareback Pads

Riding bareback is an excellent way to improve your riding skills. By feeling the horse's muscles as he works, you can get better at moving with him and concentrating on the way both of your bodies move when you are riding. A bareback pad will help prevent your sliding around, since you don't have the security of a saddle. Riding bareback is best left to those who are excellent at it, because it compromises your safety in situations that can get tricky. If you're a good rider looking to improve your already independent seat, try a bareback pad.

Some bareback pads come with stirrups, but these are somewhat superfluous, because it's best to either use a saddle if you want the helpful balance of stirrups, or stick with a pure bareback pad if you are seeking to improve your independent seat.

## Hobbles

Hobbles are more common in Western barns than English ones. But once you and your horse learn how to use them, you may never go back to tying him. His first experience having his mobility so curtailed may be a little unsettling, so its best to train him to hobbles before you try to use them out on the trail.

It may be that a that a hobbled horse is more comfortable than a tied one, since he can move his head and back legs around, and is not so fixed in one position. Also, hobbling your horse helps to reduce wear and tear on the trees you find on the trail. Hobbles fit easily into a pommel or cantle bag and can be used around the barn as well as on the trail. The only drawback to hobbles is that your horse needs to learn to use them.

## Heart Monitors

If you decide to get into endurance riding, or simply want to learn more about how your horse is exerting himself, you may want a heart monitor. Its electrodes attach to the horse's girth area, and then the pulse is read on your watch.

Happy trails.

# Index